THE JOURNEY HOMEWARD

On the Road of Spiritual Reading

BOOKS BY THE AUTHOR

The Emergent Self (Co-author)

The Participant Self (Co-author)

Approaching the Sacred: An Introduction to Spiritual Reading

Steps Along the Way: The Path of Spiritual Reading

A Practical Guide to Spiritual Reading

Tell Me Who I Am: Questions and Answers on Christian Spirituality (Co-author)

The Journey Homeward: On the Road of Spiritual Reading

Susan Annette Muto

THE JOURNEY HOMEWARD

On the Road of Spiritual Reading

With a Preface by
Adrian van Kaam

DIMENSION BOOKS

Denville, New Jersey 07834

Published by DIMENSION BOOKS
Denville, New Jersey

Grateful acknowledgment is made to Doubleday & Company, Inc. for permission to quote excerpts from *The Jerusalem Bible,* Reader's Edition (New York, 1971), Copyright © 1966 by Darton, Longman & Todd, Ltd. and Doubleday & Company, Inc.; to the Institute of Carmelite Studies for permission to quote from *The Collected Works of St. John of the Cross,* translated by Kieran Kavanaugh and Otilio Rodriguez, Copyright © 1964 by Washington Province of Discalced Carmelites, Inc. Paperback edition published by ICS Publications, Washington, D.C. U.S.A.; and to Harcourt Brace Jovanovich, Inc. for permission to quote T.S. Eliot's "A Song for Simeon," from *Collected Poems* 1909-1962 by T.S. Eliot, Copyright © 1936; Copyright © 1963, 1964, by T.S. Eliot. Reprinted by permission of the publishers.

Nihil Obstat: Rev. William J. Winter, S.T.D.
Censor Librorum
Imprimatur: Most Rev. Vincent M. Leonard,
D.D. *Bishop of Pittsburgh-*
March 17, 1977

L.C.C.No. 77-79225
ISBN 0-87193-001-3

ABOUT THE AUTHOR

Susan Annette Muto, Ph.D., holds a doctorate in English Literature with a specialization in the literature of spirituality. She is assistant director of the Institute of Man at Duquesne University and coordinator of its master's program in Fundamental Catholic Spirituality. At the Institute's Center for the Study of Spirituality, she is involved with faculty and students in the study and development of a fundamental or foundational Catholic spirituality in its formative dimension. Dr. Muto is also managing editor of the Institute's monthly spiritual journal *ENVOY* and of *HUMANITAS*, the tri-yearly journal of the Institute's Center for the Study of Human Development. She teaches courses on the art and discipline of meditative reflection and spiritual reading and frequently lectures here and abroad on these and related topics.

TABLE OF CONTENTS

PART ONE
THE SPIRITUAL READER READIES HIMSELF
FOR THE JOURNEY HOMEWARD

PART TWO
THE SPIRITUAL READER
JOURNEYS HOME TO GOD

PREFACE
By Adrian van Kaam

This book by Dr. Muto crowns her trilogy on the art and discipline of spiritual reading. This work is, at the same time, an end and a beginning. It is the end of an attractive exposition of how to read the works of the masters in such a way that their wisdom and experience may touch and transform us. Once we have established in ourselves this habit of formative reading, we may use it in service of our growth and animation. It may also be the beginning of something more. For the same approach seems to be an ideal one to foster a deeper study of spiritual theology as contained not merely in manuals on this subject, which offer only abstract compilations, but first and foremost in the original writings of the spiritual masters and doctors of the Church.

An attentive reading of this last volume of her trilogy discloses already the movement of the author's thought in that direction. This movement is not surprising. Dr. Muto, an associate professor of literature and spirituality, teaches the spiritual theology of the Church as contained in the original works of the masters. Study and research in spiritual theology forms the heart and core of the program in formative spirituality of the Institute of Man at Duquesne University of which Dr. Muto is the coordinator. This function inspires her, her colleagues and students to concentrate on the study and elaboration of the theology of the spiritual masters. Her work has thus prepared her well for the writing of this trilogy and other works in preparation.

Most important for the study of spiritual theology is the prayerful, experiential, committed approach to the text of the spiritual theologians of the Church, working and writing within the long history of the journey of the Christian community towards intimacy with the Lord. We are grateful that this trilogy can at the same time serve the needs of the spiritual reader and those of the beginning student of spiritual theology.

This book, like the other two preceding it, selects and meditates upon spiritual texts from recognized Christian authors, and especially from St. John of the Cross. The truths highlighted by these writers are rendered in the language of today, making their wisdom available to all contemporary readers. Where possible, the wisdom of the masters is integrated with life experiences that are common to most of us. Each chapter ends with a beautiful prayer composed by Dr. Muto that expresses the devout feelings that may have been evoked in us by this meditative reading. Clergy, laity, and religious will find much food for reflection in these pages and ample encouragement to continue their journey homeward to the Lord.

FOREWORD

This book is the third of three volumes on spiritual reading. The first of this series, *Approaching the Sacred*, [1] was, as its subtitle indicates, an introduction to spiritual reading and a practical application of this art. The second, *Steps Along the Way*, [2] brought the reader further along the path of this practice by describing it as an art and discipline and by tracing through classical texts the ways along which various pilgrims have been led to the Divine. The purpose of this book is to join some of these pilgrims in spirit, if not in fact, on their journey homeward to God, for he is the beginning of their search and the end of all their endeavors.

Like its predecessors, this book will be divided into two main parts. In Part One, we shall consider how the spiritual reader readies himself for the journey he is about to embark upon by considering four attitudes essential in the person who searches for God as home and harbor of his restless heart. These attitudes are: seeing simply; hearing attentively; dwelling repeatedly; and waiting patiently.

Part Two will focus on the journey proper, that is, on what happens when the spiritual reader follows the pilgrim's path to God. We shall consider his meeting with "divine darkness"; his awakening from illusion; his spirit of prayer; his awareness of himself as sinner in need of forgiveness; his willingness to accept the afflictions and limits of life as messages of God's love; and finally his tasting already on earth the eternal happiness our heavenly Father holds in store for those who journey faithfully home to him.

Our quest begins with a prologue on the prodigal son, who exemplifies the journeying man and his welcome home, and ends with an epilogue on our journey's end.

Just as we welcome a guide to show us around a strange place when we are travelling, so as spiritual readers we welcome the guidance of a master whose wisdom and experience we can rely upon. Following the pattern established in *Approaching the Sacred,* we shall turn, therefore, to the words of St. John of the Cross, whose teachings on the spiritual life are recognized by the Church and whose qualifications to guide souls in their journey to God are unquestionable.[3] In a manner similar to what we did in that text, each chapter here concludes with personal reflection upon a text of St. John; from this reflection emerges the closing prayer. We refer to this final section as the "Journal of the Journey."

ACKNOWLEDGMENTS

The inspiration for this book has emerged in dialogue with the faculty, students, and staff of the Institute of Man's Center for the Study of Spirituality. To them, as well as to my family whose support I rely upon, I dedicate its contents and the heartfelt prayer that God's grace will lead them to the light of eternal joy in him. I am especially grateful to Father Adrian van Kaam, who patiently read the manuscript and offered many suggestions for its improvement.

PART ONE

THE SPIRITUAL READER READIES HIMSELF
FOR THE JOURNEY HOMEWARD

PROLOGUE

The Prodigal Son

He also said, "A man had two sons. The younger said to his father, 'Father, let me have the share of the estate that would come to me.' So the father divided the property between them. A few days later, the younger son got together everything he had and left for a distant country where he squandered his money on a life of debauchery.

"When he had spent it all, that country experienced a severe famine, and now he began to feel the pinch, so he hired himself out to one of the local inhabitants who put him on his farm to feed the pigs. And he would willingly have filled his belly with the husks the pigs were eating but no one offered him anything. Then he came to his senses and said, 'How many of my father's paid servants have more food than they want, and here am I dying of hunger! I will leave this place and go to my father and say: 'Father, I have sinned against heaven and against you; I no longer deserve to be called your son; treat me as one of your paid servants.' So he left the place and went back to his father.

"While he was still a long way off, his father saw him and was moved with pity. He ran to the boy, clasped him in his arms and kissed him tenderly.

Then his son said, 'Father, I have sinned against heaven and against you. I no longer deserve to be called your son.' But the father said to his servants, 'Quick! Bring out the best robe and put it on him; put a ring on his finger and sandals on his feet. Bring the calf we have been fattening, and kill it; we are going to have a feast, a celebration, because this one of mine was dead and has come back to life; he was lost and is found.' And they began to celebrate.

"Now the elder son was out in the fields, and on his way back, as he drew near the house, he could hear music and dancing. Calling one of the servants he asked what it was all about. 'Your brother has come' replied the servant, 'and your father has killed the calf we had fattened because he has got him back safe and sound.' He was angry then and refused to go in, and his father came out to plead with him; but he answered his father, 'Look, all these years I have slaved for you and never once disobeyed your orders, yet you never offered me so much as a kid for me to celebrate with my friends. But, for this son of yours, when he comes back after swallowing up your property—he and his women—you kill the calf we had been fattening.'

"The father said, 'My son, you are with me always and all I have is yours. But it was only right we should celebrate and rejoice, because your brother here was dead and has come to life; he was lost and is found.' "[1]

REFLECTION

This parable of Jesus offers the spiritual reader a succinct illustration of the journey homeward. The story is simple enough. A young man from a well-to-do family asks his father to give him the inheritance now that he knows is due him later. The father agrees, against his best judgment, and shortly after the son goes away to seek his fortune. Instead, in a fashion typical of irresponsible youth, he wastes his money on frivolous pleasures, "on a life of debauchery." Out of money and in a country suffering famine, he felt the pangs of starvation and poverty. What would he do now? He had to have some money so he took the only job he could find: feeding pigs. In fact the situation was so bad that he even envied the husks they were eating.

Then, the narrative says, he came to his senses. He saw what was going on. How could he be so blind? Why his father's servants were better off than he! He lost all pride at that point, all bold self sufficiency, and knew there was only one choice left. He had to humble himself before his father, ask forgiveness for his sins, and go home. What he never suspected was the welcome that would await him. Were he in his father's shoes, he would have judged harshly, but his father's heart softened as soon as he saw his son. Jesus says he "ran to the boy, clasped him in his arms and kissed him tenderly." His son was confessing his sins and his father could only respond by preparing a feast in his honor.

What a wonderful homecoming it was. A celebration as joyful as that which occurs when we lose something precious and find it again. All was not perfect, however. Imagine how his older brother must have felt. We would be upset, too. Here he was—loyal to his father, always at his side, never disobeying—and all that goodness was taken for granted! How dare his father treat that good-for-nothing with such grace! Didn't he have any sense of justice? Only now can Jesus make his point.

When it comes to welcoming home the lost son who is humble and contrite of heart, this human father, like our heavenly Father, is at that moment full of mercy. With justice he condemns. He does not condone what his son did. He cherishes the obedience of the older brother. But his heart goes out in mercy to that second son who recognizes he has sinned and begs for forgiveness. It is right to celebrate and rejoice, says Jesus, because what was dead has come to life, what was lost has been found.

Such is the story of our homecoming to the Father. Like the younger son, we too are tempted to seek our fortune outside the flock he has chosen. We too expect to find truth elsewhere. Our pride takes over. We too feel we can make it without his protection. We want to be independent. We don't need God. We can make it on our own. The story of the younger son may repeat itself. Material goods may disappear. Other homes may cease to welcome us. Our so-called friends may desert us. We are quite alone, tasting no longer the good food of our father's table, but only the bitter flavor of our own failure. Then, again, we may not experience the loss of earthly goods, of success and status; yet we may begin to experience a loss of inner peace and contentment. We are no longer satisfied with all these possessions. We begin to feel restless inwardly. We ask ourselves: is that all?

Qoheleth

At this moment of inner deprivation, of ego desperation, we can sink further in our worldly attachments or come to our senses. Coming to our senses means reflecting on the reality of our situation: seeing where we have come from, where we are now, where we are going. Coming to our senses means acknowledging our separation from our ultimate good and begging to be taken back into our Father's graces. On this decision rests our conversion from one stony of heart, boldly self-reliant, to one pliable of heart, meekly repentant. In this state of sorrow, humbled by failure and recognizing our need for redemption, we can begin the journey homeward.

The psalmist tells us that God does not scorn the humble and broken of heart. [2] He is there to put back together the pieces of a life our proud plans have reduced to shambles. He meets our contrition with mercy, our confession with reconciliation. He loves those who remain at home with him, provided they do not become proud. But he seems especially to welcome those whose hearts have been humbled by failure. The quality of their love and faith takes on a new intensity. They know what it's like to be back home because they have been so far away. His word becomes for them a new source of inspiration. They are likely now to listen with a keenness of ear they never had before. They want to dwell in his house, absorbing the treasures of truth that lie within.

Each of us in his own way can identify with the prodigal son. Each of us has probably strayed from the Way and the Truth at one time or another. Each of us has known the failure of self-centered plans. Perhaps our hearts have been humbled. If so, we are already on the way to that union with the Father which this book intends to affirm. We are already on the way to dwelling on his word and journeying home to God.

CHAPTER ONE

Seeing Simply

To ready ourselves for the journey homeward, we, as spiritual readers, ask for the grace to grow in the attitude of seeing simply. Simple means, among other things, uncomplicated, lacking in guile, being like a little child. Seeing simply refers for our purposes to several attitudes that aid spiritual reading. These attitudes are related to one another; they include: seeing beyond the literal meaning of the text to its message for us; seeing with eyes of faith the Invisible Good we seek to be awakened to in spiritual reading; seeing the light that leads us as readers through the dense forest of confusion and doubt to the radiant vision of God's wisdom and truth. Briefly, this first preparatory step for the journey homeward implies on the part of the reader seeing not only the immediate, obvious meaning of the text but its inner depth; seeing with eyes of simple faith the One we seek to follow; seeing his timeless truths revealed again and again in the testimony of spiritual texts. Let us look at each of these phases of seeing simply in turn.

Seeing More Than the Literal Meaning

When we do spiritual reading, we soon become aware that a distinction has to be made between what we would call the "first clearness" and the "second clearness."[1] First clearness refers to the obvious or literal meaning we must look for when we read a spiritual master. On first reading we try to grasp what the writer meant to say, for example, about silence or speaking, time or eternity, action or detachment. We soon find out, however, that we as spiritual readers cannot be content with this first clearness. It is not enough to know merely what the text should obviously mean to any serious reader; we want also to discover what it says personally to us. What message might the Holy Spirit be trying to convey by the mediation of this word? We look, therefore, for a second clearness; we look beyond the obvious, general meaning of the text to its message for us.

Before this personal message begins to reveal itself, we might experience a kind of chasm. As cursory clarity wanes, what follows is often confusion or dryness—the feeling that we do not really understand as much as we thought we did or that nothing speaks to us in a really personal way. We experience a loss of confidence in our ability to translate the meaning we have grasped into a message we can apply to our lives here and now. Paradoxically, when this dryness is felt, it may be a sign that we are moving into the deep matters being discussed by the spiritual master.

For example, when we read the writings of St. John of the Cross, we may with some effort be able to outline the main stages of the ascent to God as he sees them. Before long, we may understand intellectually what he is writing about. But this is not enough. Now begins the real labor of spiritual reading, which is more than an exercise of the ego intelligence. It calls upon us to go beyond the literal clarity of the text and to immerse ourselves in its message for our spiritual life. At this point we may become disturbed. We start to question our complacency. Have we really undergone radical conversion? Are we afraid to live in the darkness of faith? Are we able to remain in God's presence with loving attention? Such questions invite us to go beyond the first to the second clearness; we want, in other words, to see what God is trying to say to us in these thought-provoking words.

This second clearness may lead us to see ourselves, as it were, mirrored in the text. There we stand in all our poverty and false pride, intending God's will but so frequently choosing our own. Out of this seeing, however painful, may stem the option for self transformation that is the gift of personalized reading. Such reading plunges us below the surface of the text to its transforming depths. It requires that we step out of the pressures of day-to-day life, if only for a while, and begin consciously to search for life's deepest meaning. This choice says in effect that we are willing to listen to the Father whenever and however he chooses to speak to us through his Holy Spirit. Despite the risk of self humiliation, we want to see ourselves as we are in the mirror of the master's text. We try to accept the revelation of our weakness calmly. Seeing the inroads of our self deception and the frequency of our failure can be an occasion for lifting our hearts to God in profound surrender. What follows from this seeing ought to be a gentle attempt to will peacefully the improvement God's grace allows, not a violent effort to attain instant perfection.

When we take up the text of a spiritual master like St. John more seriously and in a prayerful presence, something tells us that we cannot easily dismiss it on first reading, that it may touch us deeply. Having opted to follow the pilgrim's path to God, we feel in need of sound guidance; we ask for the grace to make our own the profound insights the text conveys. We feel inclined to go back to the words of the master because we know they contain basic wisdom about the spiritual life that can form and transform our own. The text can teach us to see the Way we are to follow if we want to journey home. It can simplify our seeing so that we do not get sidetracked from our goal: a life of intimacy with the Indwelling Trinity. To follow this path, we need to pass from the first to the second clearness. The Holy Spirit invites us through the mediation of the text to see the hidden depths of this mysterious love-relation between God and man. Only on this profound level can grace clarify our vision enough to enable us to greet the God who wills our good every step of the way.

Seeing the Good We Seek to be Awakened To

Spiritual masters tell us that during this brief span of time that is ours on earth, we need to reflect on our finitude. When we see everyday things against the end point of earthly life, they take on an aura of mystery. Simple objects like boots or books, man-made inventions like bridges and buildings, natural gifts like birds and bees seem to possess a mysterious hidden dimension of meaning. What holds all these things in being, myself included? I experience that I am not their source nor the source of myself. I and all that is seem wholly dependent on some Invisible Good, who is the source and sustainer of all that is given. I am not the giver but the receiver of these many gifts, my own life included.

When surface vision recedes, we may be able to open our eyes to the sustaining ground from which all that is gift emerges. We see the ground of this gift and it is good. Seeing with the eyes of faith simple things opens us to their true nature as gift. The oldest of the old—soil and sun, grain and grass—becomes the newest of the new. Seeing simply occasions a return to the origin of things, to the Creator who looked upon his handiwork and saw that it was good. To look at creation and see the good is not always easy. This goodness seems hidden amidst worldly clutter. The complex is available for view. The simple needs to be rediscovered. The complex is readily found. The simple calls for a disciplined eye.

An Eastern master wanted to teach his disciples to see the simple goodness of all things and the Mystery that invades them.² They stayed with him for a long time. They could feel how much experience the master had. What peace exuded from him as he sat in quiet contemplation of a flower, a twig, a twittering bird. What did he see that they missed? He used a few words to convey his experience, a few gestures to display the goodness he beheld, but most of the time he just sat with his disciples, not saying or doing anything. The strange thing was that this experience of just sitting with him had a powerful effect on them. They learned this practice of sitting themselves. They learned how to sit and be still and, while sitting, a few of them saw the simple. They saw into the essence of things and, like the master, they saw that the One is infinitely good.

Spiritual reading can become a practice similar to "just sitting" when we do it rightly. It can lead us toward contemplation of the good that attracts us, provided that we get involved in and stay with the text we are reading. We have to immerse ourselves in the words of the master and pause frequently to look in their light on our day-to-day experience. We have to stay with what we are reading rather than rushing from text to text if we want to absorb its full richness. Attending to the text in this way fosters in us a renewed enthusiasm for pursuing the Invisible Good in all our endeavors. By staying with the text of our choice, we learn to appreciate its message as a gift to be treasured, not as something to be hastily read and discarded. Respect for the text in its gift dimension teaches us to read not merely to gain more information but to grow in gratitude for all that has been given. Seeing simply in this light means being at once deeply thankful because we too are bound to the Invisible Good behind life's many gifts, and being quietly accepting because he calls us to celebrate what is there without trying willfully to change it.

This combination of deep gratitude and relaxed acceptance is a fine twosome to bring to spiritual reading, for there our aim is to thank God for speaking to us and to accept the path he has chosen for us. To this practice I bring my unique limits and potentials. God calls me in my uniqueness to seek and follow his goodness. I have a special part to play in his divine symphony, as the following experience may illustrate.

A student of mine described a summer experience by the shore that illumines this goal of grateful acceptance. He was sitting on the warm sand, enjoying the beauty of sea and sun, basking under a blue, cloudless sky. He began thinking of how everything hung together in perfect accord. Then he did a kind of mental trick; he tried to mix these elements up in a chaotic, colorful, intertwined but totally unorganized swirl of sea, sand and sky, as if they were ingredients in a fast speeding blender. The effect was frightening. The more he tried to blend all these gifts together, the more chaotic his mixture became. There was a riot of form and color but no order. Nothing hung together. Imaginatively he had to shut his blender off and pour the contents out. He had to let the parts return to being what they were: not a shapeless blend but an ordered connection of everything with everything else. All these elements are held in being by a caring Someone. All fulfill their proper end in a symphony of beauty and goodness. He experienced then a gifted moment of wonder. He got a fresh glimpse into the essential coherence, the simple togetherness of all things. He felt at one with the wholeness of life, molded by a Loving Hand. He was not a mere observer of isolated fragments thrown haphazardly together but a participant in a pattern of Providential Care, whose Divine Origin he had briefly glimpsed.

Such insights simplify our lives, making utterly irrelevant all that previously complicated them. In this attitude we are led toward the loving God who is the Invisible Origin of all this Good, whose presence guides our journey to him. This goal is what we seek repeatedly in spiritual reading. We learn through this practice to reappreciate the truth of God already given in the message of the master. Seeing the good and following its directives does not cramp our potential; it allows us to find the true nature of our being and the goal of our becoming in union with God.

Seeing God's Truth Revealed in the Text

When we are able to dwell upon the wondrous connection of all things, to accept our lack of control, to affirm our utter dependence, we may see the truth of who we are and the truth of who God is. We accept our creatureliness and adore him as our Creator and Father, as the Loving Guide who wills our good and wants us with him. This discovery of self in relation to God is understandably a life-long task. To walk in the truth of who we are and who he is is not an easy road to follow, but it can be facilitated by the witness we find in spiritual texts.

The master helps us to see all things as manifestations of the Divine, who is both in them and infinitely beyond them. For instance, St. John teaches us to dwell upon God's "traces" in all things.

> God created all things with remarkable ease and brevity, and in them He left some trace of Who He is, not only in giving all things being from nothing, but even by endowing them with innumerable graces and qualities, making them beautiful in a wonderful order and unfailing dependence on one another. All of this He did through His own Wisdom, the Word, His only begotten Son by Whom He created them.[3]

By turning our eye toward these "traces" of God in creation, St. John teaches us to abide in the wonder of his wisdom, in the splendor of his creative Word. He invites us in effect to become as little children, trusting less our rationalizing intellect and more the adoring look of love that says, "I am your child; you are my Father. I care for you, knowing that you cared for me first and for every manifestation of your love on earth."

Seeing the truth of who we are and who God is implies also that we pay attention to what the text tells us about detachment. In one of his *Sayings of Light and Love,* St. John states, "If you purify your soul of attachment to and desire for things, you will understand them spiritually. If you deny your appetite for them, you will enjoy their truth, understanding what is certain in them."[4] He seems to say that if we detach ourselves from things for their own sake and from our desire to possess them as sources of ultimate fulfillment, we will come to understand them spiritually, that is, as manifestations of God's creative Word. The benefit of detachment is better seeing. We become centered in God's truth as Creator instead of losing ourselves in the created. Centered in him, we sense his presence in all things. The created leads us to him instead of snatching us from him. Such seeing makes us more worshipful. We stand in awe before his world. Its mystery and majesty astounds us. We see at once God's otherness as Creator and his nearness as Lover. We affirm his distinctness from his creatures while celebrating his communion with them. This worshipful attitude, far from taking us out of this world, far from lessening our efficiency, enables us to be even more present and productive. Living in the light of his truth, we are less tense and uptight; we can flow with the situation and do what God asks.

The text of the spiritual master serves this unfolding revelation of God's word in creation; it confirms the wisdom and truth of his word in Jesus; and it imprints on our hearts the living mystery of his love for us. To read this word reverently makes us eager to be his disciples in this world until he calls us home to him in everlasting splendor.

Journal of the Journey

". . . we belong more to that infinite Good than we do to ourselves."[5]

†

What wisdom there is in this simple phrase of St. John's! I belong to God more than I do to myself. To belong to someone means to be so loved and cherished by him that nothing can separate the two of you. Lovers say they belong to one another. Is it so strange, then, to belong to God, who is love? The challenge is to live out of this belonging. To be freed from the demands of the ego self with all its fickle moods. To be freed for worshipping God in every event of life. To slow down and be patient. To do the best I can. To remember that when I fail, he understands and wants to forgive.

Truly, God takes tender care of his belongings and I

belong to God. When his belongings become torn, he sees that they are swiftly mended. When they are stolen by someone, he sends his Holy Spirit to recall them home. When those who belong to him try to make it on their own, he sends them the blessing of defeat. How desirous they are then to rely on his redeeming love! It is an undeserved gift to belong to God, to enjoy his nearness. It is something that happens whether I will it or not, for I am his creature. Am I truly grateful for this gift? If so, I must grow more and more like him, seeing simply the One my soul seeks, following that Infinite Good wherever he leads.

***

CLOSING PRAYER

If my soul is seeking you, O Lord,
How much more is it me you're seeking?
You give me grace
To resist mere worldly gain
And be your own disciple.
You give me faith
To rise above my weakness
And be with you in worship.
Of myself I merit no favor,
But you judge me infinitely worthwhile.
Freely, generously, graciously,
You awaken me from slumber
And never tire of calling.
You give me, amidst complexity,
The splendor of the simple,
The splendor of your word.
You let me read your message
Beneath all other meanings.
The goodness of your word
Is everywhere revealed—
And no where seen more clearly
Than in the One Beloved,
Your only Son, Our Lord.
Whatever worth I am
Is due to your own presence in me.
I am your belonging,
Called forth to serve
Until you call me home.

CHAPTER TWO

Hearing Attentively

The spiritual reader is a disciple of the word. As such he listens attentively to what the text is saying. He is interested especially in the message Holy Scripture and classical texts in the literature of spirituality can convey, for he realizes that these words have the power to transform his heart. He feels that his faith will grow if he has ears to listen to the words of the Divine Master and a heart courageous enough to follow his call.

Hearing attentively complements what we have been considering in regard to seeing simply, for it too is an attitude that readies us as spiritual readers for the journey home to God, the ground and goal of all our listening. What motivates us most deeply to hear and heed his will is our love for the Divine Master, who leads us home along the way of words. He tells us through revelation what we must do to develop inner ears—ears that listen to the Father's will and submit humbly to what he asks. Such listening places us on the road to union with the Triune God. After a lifetime of listening, we are ready to go home to the place the Father has prepared for those who love him.

Developing Inner Ears to Hear God's Word

Among the many aids to more intense listening, two seem to stand out. These are quieting the mind and growing in faith. The first fosters a freeing of reflection from the narrow confines of the analytical intelligence. The second opens the whole of my situated being to God's word while I am engaged in spiritual reading or simply present to his will in daily events.

The need for stilling the mind, for quieting our analytical intelligence, is essential when we do spiritual reading. A text from the Prologue of *The Spiritual Canticle,* for instance, may only begin to speak when we are able to let subside our analytical approach to it and quietly abide with the words of the master, whether we understand precisely what he is trying to say or not. St. John himself confesses an inability to express adequately all the meaning contained in the stanzas that make up his song.

> Since these stanzas, then, were composed in a love flowing from abundant mystical understanding, I cannot explain them adequately, nor is it my intention to do so. I only wish to shed some general light on them, since Your Reverence has desired this of me. I believe such an explanation will be more suitable. It is better to explain the utterances of love in their broadest sense so that each one may derive profit from them according to the mode and capacity of his spirit, rather than narrow them down to a meaning

unadaptable to every palate. As a result, though we give some explanation of these stanzas, there is no reason to be bound to this explanation. For mystical wisdom, which comes through love and is the subject of these stanzas, need not be understood distinctly in order to cause love and affection in the soul, for it is given according to the mode of faith, through which we love God without understanding Him. [1]

The key words here are: ". . . through which we love God without understanding Him." In learning to listen with inner ears, our attempts to *figure out* the text must give way to a *feeling for* what is being said on a more profound level than the rational mind can grasp. This is the level of love and trust. We trust that something beneficial for our spiritual life is being said here, even though we may not "get it" fully. By quieting our analytical mind, we may release inner forces of reflection that will give us a far deeper understanding than ego intelligence alone can derive.

How this inflow of deeper understanding occurs is a mystery, for such stilling does not mean a loss of analytical intelligence as such. It means simply that we have to distance ourselves from time to time from mere rational knowing in order to open ourselves to another kind of knowing, "through which we love God without understanding Him." Love moves us from knowledge we can gain on our own to the secret wisdom, the "mystical understanding" only God can give. The journey to his "inner chambers" is accomplished not through our knowing who he is, as we know a mathematical proof, but through our believing in him and loving him in a way that goes beyond what reason can grasp.

Such listening, situated in the darkness of not knowing, calls for a suspension, at least momentarily, of our usual ways of knowing and thinking. This suspension requires that we let go of whatever images we have of God so that we can place ourselves in his presence as mystery and be ready to hear his voice in the center of our being. It would be a mistake to conclude that this suspension of our usual way of knowing makes us become merely passive receivers of reality, up in the clouds of transcendence and no longer in touch with the immediate. Actually the opposite is true.

Quieting the mind, with its consequent growth in love and trust, helps us, if anything, to know more fully what is going on. This kind of listening with the inner ear absorbs us in God. It allows us to hear in the immediate message of daily reality the voice of transcendent nearness; it grants us greater awareness of the situation as the concrete line over which God communicates his will; it leads us to heed the present circumstances as possible conveyors of providential concern. Listening on this level thus reveals a vein of meaning far richer than any our isolated ego could discern.

St. John says that this love and affection in the soul

are "given according to the mode of faith." Growing in faith is a natural companion to listening in love. Faithful presence to God's word, wherever and however he speaks, helps us to hear what he is asking in each situation. Guided by faith, we are less likely to be trapped by our first quick reaction to a text. Whether God grants us consolation in reading or "allows aridity," we believe that he only wills what is for our best good. St. John confirms this belief when he says: "Neither is the sublime communication nor the sensible awareness of His nearness a sure testimony of His gracious presence, nor is dryness and the lack of these a reflection of His absence."[2] As disciples of the Incarnate Word and his inspired word, we do not live always and only on a high plane of elation but also in the events of everyday.

Faithful listening teaches us that God may be as present to us in his apparent absence as in the sensible awareness of his nearness. It makes us less bound to our narrow expectations of what should be and more present to the situation as coming from his hand. As we attend faithfully to the word of God, we begin to know, in a way that transcends mere factual knowledge, what way our Divine Master wants us to follow. Though such listening may at times leave us estranged from our familiar self and lonely, this pain is a small price to pay for the privilege of making a journey to the "deep thickets" of his consuming love.

Listening Places Us on the Road to Union

Listening to God's word in love and faith places us on the road to union with the Triune God. Being on the way does not mean being at our journey's end, for there is much to do if we want to go on hearing God's word and cooperating with its directives. Several modes of cooperation are characteristic of the pilgrim walking this path. For instance, a kind of wordless longing for union wells up spontaneously from us to him. We want to obey freely and joyfully whatever the Lord asks us to do or endure. We pray for the grace not to give up hope no matter how seemingly hopeless life becomes. Related to these directives is the one we want to focus on, a directive given in many spiritual texts as well as in Holy Scripture: that of self emptying.

Our model for "kenosis" is Christ himself.[3] St. Paul tells us in his letter to the Philippians that we must in our minds be the same as Christ Jesus:

His state was divine,
yet he did not cling
to his equality with God
but emptied himself
to assume the condition of a slave,
and became as men are;
and being as all men are,
he was humbler yet,
even to accepting death,
death on a cross.[4]

To imitate Christ in this self-emptying act, we must gradually and gently let go of ego-centered drives, needs and desires, of all that secretly or overtly tends to obstruct the workings of grace within us. Such self emptying does not happen overnight. It involves a slow process of tempering selfish desires, of reaching out to others in care and concern, of seeking not our own glory but God's.

St. John expresses his understanding of self-emptying in *The Ascent of Mount Carmel.* He writes:

> Endeavor to be inclined always:
>   not to the easiest, but to the most difficult;
>   not to the most delightful, but to the harshest;
>   not to the most gratifying, but to the less pleasant;
>   not to what means rest for you, but to hard work;
>   not to the consoling, but to the unconsoling;
>   not to the most, but to the least;
>   not to the highest and most precious, but to the
>   lowest and most despised;
>   not to wanting something, but to wanting nothing;
>   do not go about looking for the best of temporal
>   things, but for the worst,
>   and desire to enter into complete nudity,
>   emptiness, and poverty in everything in the world.[5]

These directives are not meant to be easy, for they are pointing to the necessity of inner detachment from self-centered gain, a detachment that frees us for Christian giving. We want to do just the opposite: choose the easiest; bask in the delightful; be the one who is consoled, liked, and praised; get the best out of life; grow rich in material goods. Much that is in us (vital desires, ego pride, self-actualizing tendencies) balks at these counsels; we don't want to accept the Cross, but the road to union is the road of the Cross and no sincere traveller can escape it.

This active effort at emptying does not in and by itself lead us into the deepest realms of divine intimacy. Such an experience is due wholly to grace. We do, however, proceed along the road of union by acts of loving attention to God, by offering the Prayer of the Publican ("God, be merciful to me, a sinner"), by silencing our words so that he may speak.[6] Such spiritual practices flow from the desire to empty ourselves of self-centered tendencies and enter into the inmost chambers of God's presence. At moments of profound communion, he may deign to grant us a glimpse of our journey's goal; this glimpse encourages us to go on reading, reflecting and doing whatever grace prompts us to do to facilitate this journey, though it belongs to God's initiative to bring this quest to closure.

Listening Readies Us for the Place God Has Prepared

This whole process of hearing God's word, of listening to his will, readies the journeying soul for the place God has prepared for those who love him. Gradually our whole style of life becomes one of at-

tending to the word. The divine words of Holy
Scripture, the devout words of spiritual texts, tell the
disciple to free his soul from willful attachment to
temporal things and abide in openness to the Eternal.
This message he gladly heeds. Since the road of
renunciation leads to inner liberation, the disciple is
eager to take it. He is impatient for this transforming
process to begin. He prays for the grace to be led along
the unique path the Divine Master has chosen for at-
homeness with him.

The journeying soul, despite his ardent zeal, is
aware that the way in all its details will not be revealed
at once. Going to the place God has prepared involves
a few leaps but most often a long process of growth in
wisdom, insight and experience. However well-
meaning a disciple may be, he does not always take
the right road. Years may go by before he develops the
keen ear that facilitates the right appraisal of the
divine message. Often he mistakes God's voice for his
own. Pride poses as humility. Another's progress is
envied. Discouragement stalks him. He can trust,
however, that God knows he is trying. He loves to see
his disciples on the way and help always comes when
they ask for it.

For example, when we are in danger of faltering,
the Holy Spirit may lead us to a certain passage in
Scripture or to the counsels of spiritual masters
imbued with the wisdom of the Church.[7] We may

hear the exact word we need to put us back on the true path. Some examples from St. John's *Sayings of Light and Love* are these:

> God values in you an inclination to aridity and suffering for love of Him more than all possible consolations, spiritual visions, and meditations.[8]
>
> Well and good if all things change, Lord God, provided we are rooted in You.[9]
>
> What you most seek and desire you will not find by this way of yours, nor through high contemplation, but in much humility and submission of heart.[10]
>
> The soul that journeys to God, but does not shake off its cares and quiet its appetites, is like one who drags a cart uphill.[11]

Reading and reflecting upon these counsels may relieve our discouragement, reconfirm our intention to follow the way, and prompt our return if we lose it.

As we cultivate a "hearing heart," we remember not only these but other words that offer needed guidance.[12] We remember that if we love him, it is because he has breathed his own Spirit into our being. Long before our earthly journey began, he prepared a place for us in his kingdom. We may seek him but it is only because he never ceases pursuing us. The seeker becomes the one sought. The one who has listened is now spoken to. The message, once clouded, is suddenly clear. The home long desired is finally found.

O lamps of fire!
In whose splendors
The deep caverns of feeling,
Once obscure and blind,
Now give forth, so rarely, so exquisitely,
Both warmth and light to their Beloved.[13]

+

These words are mysterious, deep and obscure. I listen to them without at first comprehending. I repeat softly this stanza. Without understanding all that it says, I feel myself slowly descending into those deep caverns of feeling. The lamps of fire seem to refer to the light of the Spirit within me. If his light is in me, why then, does it seem to grow dim? Is it because I am not ready to renounce all selfish desires in faithfulness to his will?

When I bind my hopes to anything less than God, I remain blind—as blind to him as when I willfully turn from his commands and obstinately refuse to listen. The truths of God recede when I busy myself with inner apologies for my lack of generosity. His words fall on deaf ears when I remain the focus of my own desires, forgetting that what my soul longs for is not self but him.

I refuse to listen when I fail to dispose myself to the gifts of the Spirit God graciously gives. I go from darkness to deeper darkness until the light of grace dawns within me. His grace makes possible the transformation of my stubborn soul. Then the lamp of my human willing is enflamed with the fire of his will for me. Then the caverns of feeling, in perfect accord with God's will, give forth warmth and light to my Beloved.

No visions, no voices, no extraordinary events accompany this listening. What may be given is simply the quiet mutual presence of lover and Beloved. The grace for this union is God's to give. It is his gift and he may or may not give it, just as I may or may not respond. I obstruct this gift when I cling foolishly to worldly pleasures instead of seeking what God wills.

Strangely, it is this lag in listening that may prepare my soul for union with him. Failure to hear and the unhappy consequences that follow may prompt me to acknowledge my total dependence on God alone. Once I allow him to take the lead, I have only to follow his word. I have only to try, with his unfailing help, to root out the tendrils of self-sufficiency and learn the wisdom of surrender. [14]

* * *

CLOSING PRAYER

Lord, you ask for my attention
While I grow more distracted.
Guide my actions and my life
Despite my human weakness.
When worldly ways take over,
Grant the grace of sweet return
To the road I want to follow.
Be patient when I falter,
Call me back before your altar
To the One I long to love.
Only when I listen
Can I learn to be submissive.
Otherwise selfish expectations
Mar my best intentions.
Seductive domination
Replaces self donation.
The trap of betrayal
Snaps before I know it.
Teach me, Lord, the lesson of kenosis.
Make my whole being
An embodiment of your love.
Without you, I accomplish nothing.
Only when you are beside me,
Only when your Spirit guides me,
Can I listen to your word,
Can I do your Father's will.

CHAPTER THREE

Dwelling Repeatedly

Seeing simply and hearing attentively are attitudes that ready us as spiritual readers for our homecoming to the Father. To come to a deeper understanding and living of his Divine Word, we need also to develop a third attitude, and that is the capacity to dwell repeatedly on Holy Scripture and the writings of spiritual masters. The words contained in these texts manifest a mysterious depth dimension due to the fact that they express certain basic themes of spiritual deepening. Such themes as growing in simplicity, listening to the Father's will, self-emptying in humility and detachment—and many more that we could mention—are key themes in the repertoire of Christian teaching and call for repeated reflection. They are like home ports to which we return after stormy explorations on other seas. They are like center stones in a swirling pond of possible meaning.

An Eastern master tells a story that illustrates nicely the necessity of repeated dwelling on sacred texts.[1] Watch what happens, he says, when the gamekeeper puts a carp in a pond with a stone in the center and another of equal size in a pond with no stone in the center. In the pond where the stone is, the carp swims

around this marker repeatedly in even, ordered circles
and thus has its exercise without meeting resistance. It
grows fat and healthy. The carp in the other pond has
no central point around which to swim; it goes in
erratic circles, becoming emaciated in the process. In
the pond where the carp swims around and around the
stone, its movement reveals a definite pattern and
purpose; therefore, it grows. In the pond without the
stone, the carp has nothing to swim around; therefore,
it shrinks.

This story provides an interesting image of the kind
of growth that occurs when we circle again and again
around profound spiritual texts. The repetition of
timeless truths, appearing and reappearing in
Scripture and the literature of spirituality, becomes
for us like a stone in the middle of a swirling pond. We
feel the security of solid stone each time we hear
repeated a testimony to God's providential guidance
of a person's life. We feel thankful that our role as
spiritual readers is not to be innovative in a way that
pleases the proud ego but simply to repeat these truths
in faithfulness to our personal experience. Such basics
of spiritual living as seeing simply, hearing attentively,
living tranquilly must now become our own.
Repetition of these ways is not a matter of blind
conformity but of creatively appropriating the timeless
truths of spiritual deepening. Through our living of
them, we offer a new testimony to the unique love
relationship that perdures between God and man. The

words and themes that articulate this relationship point to the depth dimension of spiritual reading and suggest reasons why we should engage in spiritual repetition.[2]

Repeated Dwelling Reveals the Depth Dimension of Spiritual Reading

When we do spiritual reading on a regular basis, we soon find ourselves dwelling repeatedly on certain texts and themes. These words resonate with meaning because they touch upon profound truths; they express mysteries of the faith that cannot be absorbed in one swift reading. In his letter to the Hebrews, St. Paul suggests:

> The word of God is something alive and active: it cuts like any double-edged sword but more finely: it can slip through the place where the soul is divided from the spirit, or joints from the marrow; it can judge the secret emotions and thoughts. No created thing can hide from him; everything is uncovered and open to the eyes of the one to whom we must give account of ourselves.[3]

Because the word of God is "alive and active," every reading may open up a new possibility of discovery. We cannot tell in advance where the Divine Word will lead us. All we can do is continue faithfully the practice of spiritual reading, even if clear answers to our questions are not forthcoming. God can address us through the word but his time of speaking may not coincide with our time of need. We must pay attention to God's silence as much as to his speaking. As St. Paul says, "No created thing can hide from him." He knows our need but he may withhold his self communication for a while. This withholding should not be seen as a source of frustration but as an invitation to return again to the spiritual text. If God were to disclose the full mystery and meaning of his word all at once, we might miss the messages that emerge from repeated reading. Each time we return to the text, the door of insight may open a little more but more always remains to be discovered due to the depth dimension of the sacred word.

St. John gives us an interesting example of repeated dwelling on the word "solitude" in Stanza 35 of *The Spiritual Canticle,* which reads:

> She lived in *solitude,*
> And now in *solitude* has built her nest;
> And in *solitude* He guides her,
> He alone, Who also bears
> In *solitude* the wound of love.[4]

In his *Commentary*, St. John dwells on the many meanings of solitude emerging from this short but profound stanza. He explains two things which the Bridegroom does in this verse:

First, He praises the *solitude* in which the soul formerly desired to live, telling how it was a means for her to find and rejoice in her Beloved alone, withdrawn from all her former afflictions and fatigues. Since she wished to live in *solitude*, apart from every satisfaction, comfort, and support of creatures, in order to reach companionship and union with her Beloved, she deserved to discover the possession of peaceful *solitude* in her Beloved, in Whom she rests, alone and isolated from all these disturbances.

Second, He states that, insofar as she desired to live apart from all created things, in *solitude* for her Beloved's sake, He Himself was enamored of her because of this *solitude* and took care of her by accepting her in His arms, feeding her in Himself with every blessing, and guiding her to the high things of God. He asserts not only that He guides her, but that He does so alone without other means (angels, men, forms, or figures), for she now possesses, through this *solitude*, true liberty of spirit which is not bound to any of these means.[5]

Whether we are reading St. John's verse or commentary, we are drawn into the depth meaning of solitude as a fundamental of the spiritual life with each repetition of this word. There is something awesome in such aloneness. God is the soul's only guide. In solitude he communes with her and unites himself to her. He speaks to her solitary heart that will settle for nothing less than himself. In her aloneness, the soul begs for at oneness with him. Solitude is the means by which she will find him and rejoice in him apart from every earthly satisfaction, comfort, and support. Not bound ultimately to any finite means of fulfillment, the soul seeks her true end. Centering herself around that "inner stone" leads her not to exhaustion but to restful freedom of spirit. With this thought in mind, we can turn to some additional reasons for spiritual repetition.

Why Engage in Spiritual Repetition?

A first reason is found in St. John's *Commentary* on Stanza 36 of *The Spiritual Canticle,* where he tells how the Beloved draws the Bride more closely into the secrets of the Beloved himself, that is "deep into the thicket." "This thicket of God's wisdom and knowledge is so deep and immense that no matter how much the soul knows she can always enter it further; it is vast and its riches incomprehensible. . . . "[6] We find confirmation for this "thicket of God's wisdom" in Romans 11:33: "How rich are the depths of God— how deep his wisdom and knowledge—and how impossible to penetrate his motives or understand his methods!"

Via the road of spiritual repetition, we are drawn ever more deeply into the dense profundity of God's motives and methods. Our feelings of frustration fade into the background as we learn to enjoy God and praise him repeatedly for who he is in himself, however unfathomable his way may be to our limited view. Repeated dwelling creates inner calm. We cease anxiously trying to figure out the intricate tapestry God is weaving and rejoice in the small thread we can contribute.

This calming effect provides a second reason for spiritual repetition. The more habitual a task becomes, the more relaxed we are while doing it. For instance, when I am sewing on a button, my fingers work but my thoughts can be quietly centered in deeper matters. The sure, steady movements of wrist and hand, now that I know how to sew, contrast with those initial awkward efforts I remember so well. Repeated practice frees me from the nervous demand to master unknown factors: how to thread the needle, what size button to use, how many times to tie the final knot. The same principle applies to painting, cooking, dancing, piano playing—to all the arts. Through repeated practice, I achieve the "facility of the familiar." Now I can let flow from that familiar base a certain creative flare. Creativity implies freedom of attention from the technical know-how gained by repetition of basic moves. From this knowledge comes forth the feeling of creative release and relaxation.

Certain sports are like that, too. It's a great delight, for example, to take up my tackle box and fishing pole and to go to some quiet stream. I feel as if I'm in "home territory" and hardly have to think about what I'm doing as I bait the hook, cast, and, with luck, reel in! Through repetition, I have gained the facility to relax and enjoy this sport.

The same can be said for spiritual reading. Through the practice of this art, I become more at home with and receptive to the wisdom conveyed by the words of Scripture and spiritual masters. Repeated dwelling with the text, so to speak, "purifies my spiritual radar." As I calmly and peacefully approach my reading, a lot of disruptive static clears up and I am able to pick out the essential message that will help me to live more meditatively. By means of repetition, the inner self begins to emerge. I receive from day-after-day reading of sacred words the possibility of releasing my deepest interiority. I receive the affirmation to become who I am in God, despite the hurdles I may have to cross.

What at one point appears to be an obstacle can become, as I dwell upon it, a means to release my inner potential. While reading Holy Scripture, for example, we meet many people—Jeremiah and Paul immediately come to mind—who never thought they could overcome their weaknesses and become God's prophets—but they did. They offered him their poverty and he gave them in return great power to do good. Dwelling on texts that depict their struggle prepares us to respond calmly and courageously to whatever God asks. Seeing how others have met the challenge of their call encourages us to say yes to our own.

A third reason for learning to dwell repeatedly with the truths of spiritual living is that this dwelling leads us to stand firm in our intention to serve God. However trying the circumstances in which he places us, we intend not to betray him. True, we might fail, but failure does not mean giving up. It is simply an invitation to try again. As we grow in presence to the Divine who dwells within us, we see that it does not require extraordinary feats to draw him to us. He is with us if we turn within. Constant reaching out only creates an agitated spirit, fearful of failure and looking for spectacular ways to serve him. All such efforts may only increase his absence. We forget that God is everywhere, in all persons and situations. Repeated dwelling on his word tells us that he lives in the valleys as well as on the high places, that he is as much at home in a carpenter shop as in a monastery. He is not far away but intimately near.

This sense of *being with* him does not necessarily mean constantly *thinking about* him. Repeated dwelling implies living with him in a heart-to-heart relationship; it implies a relaxed, tension-free turning toward him and trying to sense his presence everywhere. At certain moments of meditative reading or contemplative prayer, he is "figural"; at other moments, in the midst of daily action, he is "ground." Whatever may be the case, this tranquil rhythm of contemplation and action, frequently repeated, makes room in our hearts for the Divine to enter whenever and however he chooses. Spiritual repetition thus cultivates within us, in cooperation with grace, and abiding presence to God that pervades our being and guides our doing.

A final reason for repetition as practiced in spiritual reading and living is that it keeps thought from meandering aimlessly and implants in the soul the seeds of divine remembrance. Thoughts gather around the main thought of doing his will. Memory finds traces of his providence in what seemed to be disparate events. Imagination pictures how he responded to certain situations. Will prompts us to act accordingly. In other words, what we think and imagine, say and do, takes place in light of God's presence. We repeat to ourselves again and again, we try to remember in all surroundings and events, that to him belongs the kingdom, the power, the glory. God alone is God and we are his children, made in his image, made to worship him only and not idols of our own making.

To abide daily in God's presence, to dwell repeatedly with him in word and work, is to make the journey homeward. We witness his goodness in the food we eat, the family we love, the health he grants. We celebrate his self revelation in sacred symbol, in the book of his word, in the liturgical year, in the Church he established. We see ourselves as creatures ultimately dependent on him, our Creator. Dwelling with him in total dependence means that we hold fast to God in our hearts. He is not an afterthought but the source and end of every thought.

Such an experience of union is not something we on our own can create, but we can prepare ourselves for this gift by repeated dwelling on his word. Spiritual repetition can ready us for union with the Father, but only he can lead us to lasting rest in him. This gift of union is the goal sought by all who want to journey homeward; it is the goal hoped for by the spiritual reader in all his dwelling on the word.

Journal of the Journey

My spirit has become dry because it forgets to feed on You. [7]

+

The inner life needs to be nourished at its Divine Source. Otherwise, like a withered plant or a well without water, this drying up results. If my spirit dries up, I dry up. My eyes lack lustre; my smile feels pasted on; my words sound only surface deep. My soul needs to "feed on God" if it is to reach fullest maturity. It needs the living waters of prayer and solitude, of recollection and spiritual reading, of repeated practices through which I meet the Lord and in him find new life for my soul.

Dryness may still come upon me despite dwelling frequently with his sacred word. I may feel unable to pray, inwardly arid, bored and fed up. Everything seems tasteless. When these occasions come, they have to be accepted as part of the spiritual life and

lived through in hope. Though at the moment I may
not feel God's nearness, I must continue to believe
that he is with me, aware of my predicament and
ready to offer consolation when the time is right. If I
can turn to him, no matter how I feel, the dryness will
gradually disappear and I may even feel grateful for
this desert experience.[8]

Dryness of spirit is often linked to desire—the
desire for something other than God, something that
threatens to displace him as my center. In truth, I
want my will, not his, to be done. Dryness sets in when
I try to satisfy my own will, for even if I do, this human
fulfillment always disappoints in some way. No finite
fulfillment of desires can ever satisfy my infinite desire
for God. To dwell with him, I have to give up my own
will, but this loss is, from the viewpoint of faith, infinite gain. God is found not in self-gratification but
in self-denial. Instead of bargaining with him or trying
to comprehend his ways, I must stand before him in
humility and submission of heart. Such renunciation
becomes the condition for spiritual liberation.

I recall in this regard reading *The First Circle,* a
novel by Alexander Solzhenitsyn in which he describes
the condition of the zek—a prisoner in the Russian
labor camps.[9] Solzhenitsyn shows that some men only
experience the true meaning of freedom when
everything is taken away from them, for one has
nothing left to cling to and is thus not afraid of loss. In
one sense, a slave may become the only free man. Due
to his circumstances, he becomes purged of the in-

stant fulfillment of his desires, for every wish he has may be thwarted by his captors. His spirit, no longer captivated by great desires, becomes present to the simple goods of daily life—a button, a piece of bread, a brief exchange with a fellow zek—goods that may symbolize for him higher values of the human spirit no amount of torture can destroy. Others may become the slaves of their small desires for the little things imprisonment still allows them to procure. But, in the void of worldly desire, Solzhenitsyn suggests, there may issue forth in some prisoners a hymn to inner freedom. Deprivation, instead of drying up the spirit, paradoxically may make possible a condition of transcendent dignity in those who are open to grace and the Spirit.

Only when everything temporal is taken away may the zek experience the recovery of his eternal soul. Jesus himself has said that if we do not renounce all that we possess we cannot be his disciples. Solzhenitsyn brings this point out strongly in his story of the zek who possesses nothing earthly and so becomes finely attuned to the spirit within. This transformation is evidenced in the inner peace a number of prisoners experience. The dignity that is theirs transcends these wretched circumstances. Thanks to God's grace, some have found in captivity a meaning their captors cannot take away, for no bars can bind the human spirit that soars free to God, that comes alive because it remembers to feed on him.[10]

* * *

CLOSING PRAYER

Lord, let me not forget to feed on you
Lest my spirit become dry,
Dry and arid like the desert sand,
Dissatisfied and bored trying to fulfill
My limited human will
Instead of soaring free
To follow without fear
The way of Union you've decreed for me.
Grant me the grace to withdraw periodically.
Clear my inner eyes of worldly dust
That I may see your radiant beauty everywhere.
In you all things flow as from a tranquil source.
Let me find my place in this most holy plan,
The place where I belong.
Let me live the promise of your peace
In my soul, in this land.
Plant these words like seeds within my soul.
Let them sprout like spring blooms
Fed by rain and sun.
Should I fail to feed on you,
Nourish me still with generous grace.
Let the seeds of good intention grow.
Come to my aid, for I am weak.
Without your help, given repeatedly,
I cannot begin my homeward trek
Nor hope to arrive, a pilgrim,
At your door.

CHAPTER FOUR

Waiting Patiently

As spiritual readers, we ready ourselves for the journey homeward by learning to see simply, hear attentively, and dwell repeatedly with the words of Holy Scripture and the writings of spiritual masters. We must learn also to wait patiently upon the word, should the Spirit choose to use the text as a channel of divine communication.

When we are expecting a person we love to come home, we stand before the window, eyes wide open, watching for the first sign of his arrival. We await that surge of happiness when his wave is seen over the horizon. We would not dream of moving from our watching place. We waver between patience and impatience as the clock ticks away. When will he come? Be calm. It's almost time. Yes! There he is. We run breathless toward the one who makes all that waiting worthwhile.

Compare this familiar human scene to the relationship between the soul and God, fostered by spiritual reading. The soul feels such an attraction for the things of eternity, spoken of in the text, that at times the whole universe appears valueless in comparison to the good that is to come, the good we hope

to possess everlastingly. ,We wait upon the Divine
Word, knowing that of ourselves we can never still this
restless desire for union with him. We wait like faithful watchmen in the night because we know God is
true to his word. He has assured us we shall enter into
eternal life if we love him and listen to our Lord. If we
refuse to keep his word, we cannot enter the
Kingdom. We give in to the temptation to place our
trust in earthly possession and control contrary to the
poverty and humility he asks us to bear for his sake.
The more we wait upon his word, the more we experience its power to rid us of false expectations of
what we think will fulfill us so that we may come to
rejoice in what God is offering: the gift of himself.
Slowly and gradually, we let go of the shoulds and
oughts, the nevers and musts of mere worldly life and
attend to what really matters—God's loving
possession of us and our trust in his promise of eternal
salvation.

In her book, *Waiting for God,* Simone Weil stresses
that we must not give up even in the most
discouraging situations.[1] We must continue to wait on
God with ever-increasing love and attentiveness
despite our sufferings in this life. Such waiting involves the ongoing orientation of our whole being to
the Lord. What prompts this patient waiting is not
will power but longing love. What leads us again and
again to his word is not the need for absolute certitude
but the gentle opening of ourselves to his guidance.

Waiting requires at times the suspension of our thoughts about what should be. We keep our minds empty of selfish plans, our hearts open and detached, ready to be penetrated by him who is tirelessly seeking us.

Compare this kind of waiting to what happens in the realm of creativity. The creative person may spend months mulling over a problem. A certain tension builds up. The strain he feels tells him that he has to let go of his efforts to reach a solution. Take the familiar example of solving a mathematical problem. The more the mathematician sets out impatiently to seek the answer he is looking for, the farther that answer recedes from him. All he gains are counterfeit solutions. If he can let go of his efforts to reach a quick solution and be patient, he may find the answer suddenly there. To solve the problem he has had to exercise a certain degree of concentrated thought. However, if he has not at the same time trained himself in patient waiting, he may unwittingly block the answer's sudden emergence by his aggressive effort to force its appearance.

Waiting in the spiritual order implies, therefore, being wakeful and alert but at the same time remaining in profound stillness within. We must be careful, when doing spiritual reading, not to lose our inner openness to God's word in a tangled mess of self-imposed suggestions and desires completely out of touch with his will, speaking in our concrete situation.

Learning to wait upon his word in the text complements our learning to wait upon his call in daily
life. Help will come if we humbly and unceasingly ask
for it. God's answer may not meet our expectations
but, then, he never promised us happiness in this
world. He tells of persecutions that will come. He asks
us to endure patiently the trials obedience to his word
portend. He calls us elsewhere, to another home where
the reward of waiting upon his word will far outweigh
any suffering endured.

Two Kinds of Waiting

We have been suggesting implicitly that there is a
distinction, to be fostered in spiritual reading, between "waiting for" and "waiting upon."[2] Waiting *for*
something to happen implies that I bring to my
reading a host of expectations about what the text
should be saying to me. I want to read only what
confirms my understanding of God's will here and
now. I wait frantically for spiritual consolation.
Whatever resists my willfulness wearies me. I become
discouraged when the text offers no positive response
to what I am thinking. My tendency, then, is not to
deal with this resistance but to change texts. In this
"waiting for" style of reading, what wearies me is not
the text itself but the stubborness of my will; what
builds up resistance is the host of false expectations I
have become inordinately attached to. In truth I am

waiting for the word to serve me rather than waiting upon it.

Waiting *upon* implies a different style of approach, a willingness to be with the word as its meaning unfolds for me in accordance with God's will; it implies suspending the expectation of instant consolation and blissful communion. If anything, I am prone to expect dryness and resistance as part of the experience of spiritual reading. Waiting upon the word means reaching out to its transcendent horizon, not reducing it to what I can immediately like and grasp.

In preference to the consumer mentality that shops around for consoling texts, I choose to stay with the text I have selected, especially if sections of it stir up my complacency. Waiting upon the text teaches me that I do not have all the answers. Life messages emerging from God's word require repeated reflection and the option to remain open to change, however disrupting.

Not calculating in advance precisely where the word will lead me allows me to be led where God wants me to go. I read not to *have read*—not merely to get in my allotted time of meditative reading—but to follow the path God lays out for me in the unfolding mystery of my life. The uncertainty I feel does not discourage me; it becomes an invitation to trust. In a relaxed way, I am able to say to God, "If what I expect happens, fine; if it doesn't, I accept that, too, as your will."

Waiting upon is not to be understood as being totally passive; it is rather the receiving and active acceptance of God's will wherever it may lead. The more I wait upon his word, the more I realize how foolish it is to become impatient when things do not go my way. All God allows is part of his providential care. My place is to wait upon him—not to force his hand or to expect him to conform to my short-sighted schedule.

Like Job, I too must bow to the Creator's wisdom. Of what value are my "empty-headed words" compared to those Yahweh proclaims from the heart of the tempest?

> Brace yourself like a fighter;
>   now it is my turn to ask questions and yours to in-
> form me.
> Where were you when I laid the earth's foundations?
>   Tell me, since you are so well informed!
> Who decided the dimensions of it, do you know?
>   Or who stretched the measuring line across it?
> What supports its pillars at their bases?
>   Who laid its cornerstone
> when all the stars of the morning were singing with
> joy, and the Sons of God in chorus were chanting
> praise?
> . . . .
> Have you journeyed all the way to the sources of the
> sea,
>   or walked where the Abyss is deepest?

Have you been shown the gates of Death
  or met the janitors of Shadowland?
Have you an inkling of the extent of the earth?
  Tell me all about it if you have!
Which is the way to the home of the light,
  and where does darkness live?
You could then show them the way to their proper places,
  or put them on the path to where they live!
If you know all this, you must have been born with them,
  you must be very old by now![3]

Hearing these stinging words of reproach, I feel something of Job's shame. I too have tried to make the Creator accountable to me when his wisdom transcends anything I can hope to grasp. With Job, I want to repent of these foolish expectations and wait upon the glory and majesty of God's creative and incarnate word. Job's answer to Yahweh then becomes my own.

I know that you are all-powerful:
  what you conceive, you can perform
I am the man who obscured your designs
  with my empty-headed words.
I have been holding forth on matters I cannot understand,
  on marvels beyond me and my knowledge.
(Listen, I have more to say,
  now it is my turn to ask questions and yours to inform me.)

I knew you then only by hearsay;
  but now, having seen you with my own eyes,
I retract all I have said,
  and in dust and ashes I repent. [4]

At such moments of profound repentance, I turn again to God's word as a trustworthy guide in my quest for truth. This guiding word is God's own son. I ask Jesus to let me hear the summons of the hour and to free me from whatever hinders my response.

Obstacles and Aids to Waiting Upon God's Word

The expectation of worldly success as an end in itself poses an obstacle to waiting upon God's word, as Jesus revealed so often in his public life. Again and again he showed that earthly power is not the ultimate proof of a successful life from the perspective of Christian living. The publican was dubbed a failure in the eyes of men but his prayer was more pleasing to God than that of the much honored Pharisee. Jesus knew that the success motive could lead us to serve our own will rather than the Father's. His persistent attacks on the Pharisees reveal just how much he despised their desire to make worldly success a measure of spiritual progress.

He had just finished speaking when a Pharisee invited him to dine at his house. He went in and sat down at the table. The Pharisee saw this and was surprised that he had not first washed before the meal. But the Lord said to him, "Oh, you Pharisees! You clean the outside of cup and plate, while inside yourselves you are filled with extortion and wickedness. Fools! Did not he who made the outside make the inside too? Instead, give alms from what you have and then indeed everything will be clean for you. But alas for you Pharisees! You who pay your tithe of mint and rue and all sorts of garden herbs and overlook justice and the love of God! These you should have practiced, without leaving the others undone. Alas for you Pharisees who like taking the seats of honor in the synagogues and being greeted obsequiously in the market squares! Alas for you, because you are like the unmarked tombs that men walk on without knowing it!"⁵

The Pharisees wanted to measure spiritual growth by such outward signs as giving tithes so people would see and they would be bowed to in the marketplace. They were blind to the fact that the life of the spirit concerns growth in inwardness. This deepening may go unseen by the eyes of men but it pleases God greatly. He sees progress from within. For him what counts is not outward praise but the day-after-day hiddenness of trying to live the Christian life.

"And that is why the Wisdom of God said, 'I will send them prophets and apostles; some they will slaughter and persecute, so that this generation will have to answer for every prophet's blood that has been shed since the foundation of the world, from the blood of

Abel to the blood of Zechariah, who was murdered
between the altar and the sanctuary.' Yes, I tell you,
this generation will have to answer for it all. . . ."[6]

Jesus, like the prophets of the Old Testament, chose
to be powerless in the worldly sense that he might gain
spiritual power by waiting upon his Father's will. Like
him, I, too, must choose to be a poor, powerless
disciple of the word, waiting upon it patiently, giving
it the power to change my life. This transformation
occurs not by force but by the Lord's gentle drawing
out of my best potential to praise, serve, and thank
him no matter how persecuted and despised I may be
in the eyes of the world.

The thirst for wealth poses a related obstacle to this
kind of waiting. Again Jesus willed the opposite, in
regard to hoarding possessions, he told the assembled
crowd this parable:

"There was once a rich man who, having had a good
harvest from his hand, thought to himself, 'What am
I to do? I have not enough room to store my crops.'
Then he said, 'This is what I will do: I will pull down
my barns and build bigger ones, and store all my
grain and my goods in them, and I will say to my soul:
My soul, you have plenty of good things laid by for
many years to come; take things easy, eat, drink, have
a good time.' But God said to him, 'Fool! This very
night the demand will be made for your soul; and this
hoard of yours, whose will it be then?' So it is when a

man stores up treasure for himself in place of making himself rich in the sight of God."[7]

Jesus shows us that instead of stocking high our barns with worldly goods, we need to place unconditional trust in the Father's care.

". . . Think of the flowers; they never have to spin or weave; yet, I assure you, not even Solomon in all his regalia was robed like one of these. Now if that is how God clothes the grass in the field which is there today and thrown into the furnace tomorrow, how much more will he look after you, you men of little faith! But you, you must not set your hearts on things to eat and things to drink; nor must you worry. It is the pagans of this world who set their hearts on all these things. Your Father well knows you need them. No; set your hearts on his kingdom, and these other things will be given you as well.

"There is no need to be afraid, little flock, for it has pleased your Father to give you the kingdom . . ."[8]

Waiting for worldly wealth to satisfy us always disappoints. Of what value are all these worldly goods, Jesus teaches, if by amassing them we have neglected to save our immortal souls?

The wrong kind of waiting happens not only when I pile up material riches as a substitute for spiritual growth but when I amass mental goods as well. Solutions to problems, sure predictions, unflinching prejudices become my gods. I stockpile these idols to mitigate risk and to give my ego the protection it seeks from the unknown. I try to build mental barriers against the surprises God keeps sending; I insulate my life from the risk of total obedience to the Father's will even when, like Jesus in his final hour, I feel utterly forsaken. Then I know the true purpose of waiting upon his word: it is to make me aware of how poor I am, to strip me of ego pretenses, to show me that the source of my wealth and well-being is to be found only in relation to my God.

Waiting upon the word also frees me to see the exquisite value of the simplest things (lilies of the field, birds of the air) because these things are God's gifts. If I can wait upon them with reverence, I may see shining through their surface appearances the inner depths of meaning Jesus wanted me to see. A friend of mine refers to this reverential waiting upon things as "seeing small." Once she was making an eastern-oriented retreat. The retreatants were asked for that week to engage in modest fasting by eating less for breakfast and dinner. Lunch was the middle and main meal of the day. The food served then was fresh and good. There was not a lot of it, so what was prepared and served was really appreciated. What happened to her involved an awakening from the "waiting for" attitude of taking food for granted to the "waiting upon" attitude of being present in gratitude to the wonder of what was on the table before her.

My friend was sitting crosslegged in the dining area on a little blanket. The food was served while she and her fellow retreatants waited. A pot of soup. A loaf of bread. A bowl of fruit. Each person had his portion. That day the cooks had made fresh bread with whipped butter and honey on the side. It was a delicious combination. She spread the butter and honey thick on the bread. She felt quiet and reflective. She held her bread reverently and slowly took a bite out of it. She swallowed the bite as she ordinarily did. Then she turned to look at her bread. She was attentive to it. She noticed, as if for the first time, her teeth marks cutting through the bread and butter. A perfect half moon bite. She thought in a flash that what was outside her a moment ago was now inside, nourishing her, sustaining her, keeping her alive. A whole horizon of meaning burst forth—that of the nurturing, sustaining, upholding mystery of nature. The grain and the wheat, the making of bread and butter, the eating of this mixture to stay alive. Like a snow ball rolling downhill, meaning upon meaning flashed in her mind. Illumined for her all at once was the mystery dimension of life. Many things were made clear in that one wordless experience. The taken-for-granted ways in which she ate food normally just to get fed were gone. What was left behind was a vivid moment of gratitude and deep trust in the Giver of all this good before whose glory she felt a humble servant.

Waiting upon the Lord in little things ("seeing small") thus illumines the present moment as a pointer toward our ultimate end—union with the Source of this mystery. The present prompts us to see behind the given the One who gives. We no longer wait for what is going to happen; we wait upon what is happening right now. Before us the greatest mysteries are unfolding if we have the faith to witness them. Patient waiting frees us from the unrealistic attempt to force circumstances to go our way; it readies us for the immediate as a revelation of the transcendent. It keeps us on the right path of humble presence to the Father's will; it gives us the confidence we need to journey homeward, however rocky the road may be.

Journal of the Journey

Bridle your tongue and your thoughts very much, direct your affection habitually toward God, and your spirit will be divinely enkindled.

Feed not your spirit on anything but God. Cast off concern about things, and bear peace and recollection in your heart.

Keep spiritually tranquil in a loving attentiveness to God, and when it is necessary to speak, let it be with the same calm and peace.

Preserve a habitual remembrance of eternal life, recalling that those who hold themselves the lowest and poorest and least of all will enjoy the highest dominion and glory in God.

Rejoice habitually in God, Who is your salvation, and reflect that it is good to suffer in any way for Him Who is good. [9]

+

In these five maxims, St. John stresses the need, if I want to arrive at spiritual deepening, for directing my affection toward God, for preserving habitual remembrance of him, for rejoicing in him—in short, for waiting upon him. When I forget the reverence due him, my perception takes in the persons and places, the things and events of this world as if God had no part in them. My attention gets absorbed in shopping or preparing classes. My thoughts center on friends or travel. While at times I may be conscious of God in the background of these activities, too often I forget about him.

The words of the spiritual master are a sharp reminder of how much I am in danger of isolating the circumstances of my life from their sustaining ground. Behind these gifts of food, clothing, social celebration, I must be ever mindful of the Giver, including him explicitly in the most mundane transactions. Were it not for his overwhelming generosity to me, I would not have the money to purchase good food or the intelligence to prepare a class.

I must wait upon these goods as signs of God's presence. Since it is unlikely that these things will be taken away, I must use them wisely—first, by never making them an ultimate concern and, secondly, by living with them without caring if I have them or not. In other words, I must learn to center my thoughts more on the Giver than on these gifts.

For instance, I arrive at my office in the quiet of the morning. Before I begin final preparations for my ten o'clock class, I ought to pause and get in touch with the day. I walk to the window and look outside. Every so often the sun breaks through. A cool breeze is blowing through the open window. It looks as if it is going to be a lovely, fall-summer kind of day. The curtains are swaying. Outside I hear the hum of traffic, inside the opening and closing of doors. Another working day, another day to be grateful for. The ordinary peacefulness of the morning conveys a message of his peace and prompts a silent prayer that it will be my own.[10]

* * *

CLOSING PRAYER

Lord, since you know me better than I know myself,
Show me the way to be at one with you.
Grant me the grace to wait upon your word
That I may love and serve you throughout all my days.
Give me patience when life fails to go my way
To wait upon the message you are trying to convey.
Teach me to be grateful for the gifts you give each day
That I may glimpse, if only momentarily,
The home you have prepared for me,
The place of peace awaiting me,
Not here but in eternity.

PART TWO

THE SPIRITUAL READER
JOURNEYS HOME TO GOD

CHAPTER ONE

Meeting With Divine Darkness

Having considered in Part One four factors that ready us as spiritual readers for the journey homeward, we are going to follow more closely in Part Two what happens as we journey along the path to divine intimacy proposed by the spiritual writer. Before long, we are likely to come across references to the "divine darkness." When spiritual masters use this phrase, or ones comparable to it, they are pointing to the ultimate incomprehensibility of God, whose mysterious essence cannot be grasped by human intellect alone. In his *Commentary* on Stanza 1 of *The Spiritual Canticle,* St. John says:

It is noteworthy that, however elevated God's communications and the experiences of His presence are, and however sublime a person's knowledge of Him may be, these are not God essentially, nor are they comparable to Him because, indeed, He is still hidden to the soul. Hence, regardless of all these lofty experiences, a person should think of Him as hidden and seek Him as one who is hidden, saying: "Where have You hidden?"[1]

The Book of Job reminds us that

> God is clothed in fearful splendor:
>   he, Shaddi, is far beyond our reach.
> Supreme in power, in equity,
>   excelling in justice, yet no oppressor—
> no wonder that men fear him,
>   and thoughtful men hold him in awe. [2]

Another witness for this "way of unknowing" that evokes awe and wonder is the anonymous author of *The Cloud of Unknowing,* a 14th Century classic of English mysticism inspired by the "dazzling darkness" theology of the Pseudo-Dionysius. [3] Like other disciples of this way, he insists that God can never be reached by conceptual knowledge, though he can be "oned with" by love. Our intellects balk at the abyss of mystery; it is only the power of loving faith that can leap across the abyss into the unapproachable light in which God dwells. It is only God himself who can bring hidden mysteries to light, who can enflesh his Divine Word. In his majesty and transcendence, he is preeminent in power and judgment. We must revere him, but however enlightened we are, we cannot see him as he is. His essential incomprehensibility escapes our analysis and so we creatures bestow upon him the name Wonder. [4]

Because the divine essence is hidden from human intellect, to encounter him requires a faith in divinely revealed truths that transcends the natural light of reason, that exceeds all human understanding. St. John counsels us to become like "blind men." We must lean on dark faith, accept it as our guide and light, and rest on nothing of what we understand, taste, feel, or imagine. All words are silenced in this loving encounter between the soul and God; we come to him in wordless adoration, abiding in the darkness of faith. The author of *The Cloud* says we must learn to be at home in this darkness, returning to it as often as we can, letting our spirit cry out to him whom we love.

Though we seem to feel nothing and to know nothing, though darkness surrounds us, the light of faith burns steadily on. St. John says this mysterious light leaves our sensory nature in darkness; we cannot touch or see the divine object of our faith. Neither can we rely on the faculty of intelligence through which we normally comprehend meaning; we cannot grasp the essence of God as we can reason through a complex equation. Though "darkening" sense perception and analytical intelligence, faith opens up new levels of seeing. It grants us a dim awareness of realities we have neither seen nor known first hand but still believe. Though faith is, in St. John's words, a "dark night" for sense and reason, this darkness gives us access to a higher kind of light. Mysteriously, the more God withdraws himself from what we can feel and from what our intellect can understand, the closer we may come to him in faith.

> To attain union with God, a person should advance neither by understanding, nor by the support of his own experience, nor by feeling or imagination, but by belief in God's being. For God's being cannot be grasped by the intellect, appetite, imagination, or any other sense, nor can it be known in this life. The most that be felt and tasted of God in this life is infinitely distant from God and the pure possession of Him.[5]

In other words, to paraphrase 1 Corinthians 2:9, no eye has seen, no ear has heard, no thought has grasped what God has prepared for those who love him.

The Dark Night of Sense

What kind of darkening is demanded of us if we want to seek intimacy with the Divine? St. John's answer is that we need in the first place to "renounce and remain empty of any sensory satisfaction that is not purely for the honor and glory of God."[6] This renunciation involves several factors that are related to one another. We are to resist the temptation to make any creature ultimate, lest we overlook our Creator; this step involves breaking off any attachment that is excessive. Denying ourselves mere sense gratification is also important; this requires that we take up our cross daily and follow Jesus, whose ultimate gratification in life was the fulfillment of his Father's will.

St. John is not condemning our senses as such. He knows that through them we can celebrate traces of God in all he has made. What he insists upon is the need to subdue the willful seeking of our own pleasure alone due to original sin. He recognizes the stark difference between the Christ-oriented self and one who is merely egocentric. True following involves the willingness to go counter to the pleasure principle, if that is what the Father asks. Therefore,

> A genuine spirit seeks the distasteful in God rather than the delectable, leans more toward suffering than toward consolation, more toward going without everything for God rather than toward possession. It prefers dryness and affliction to sweet consolation. It knows that this is the significance of following Christ and denying self, that the other method is perhaps a seeking of self in God—something entirely contrary to love. Seeking oneself in God is the same as looking for the caresses and consolations of God. Seeking God in oneself entails not only the desire of doing without these consolations for God's sake, but also the inclination to choose for love of Christ all that is most distasteful whether in God or in the world—and such is the love of God. [7]

The point here is not that I seek the distasteful in a masochistic fashion but that I maintain the inclination to choose suffering for the love of Christ if and when the Holy Spirit invites me to this renunciation. As stark as such self-denial may seem, it is exactly what Jesus did. Humanly he did not like the cross but he chose it because he loved the Father and desired deeply to obey his will. Through Christ, with him, and in him, the union between the soul and God is effected. "The journey, then, does not consist in recreations, experiences, and spiritual feelings, but in the living, sensory and spiritual, exterior and interior death of the cross."[8]

Thomas a Kempis gives us in Jesus' own words the itinerary of this journey and the demands it will make upon those who sincerely follow the crucified and risen Lord.

Willingly, with arms outstretched upon the cross where I hung naked, I offered myself to God the Father for your sins, in total surrender, my whole being turned to a sacrifice pleasing to God. So you in your turn should offer yourself to me daily at Mass, with all your powers and affections. A willing offering it ought to be, an offering pure and holy, made with all the power of your inmost heart. There is nothing I ask of you more than this, to strive to surrender yourself entirely to me. I care for nothing that you offer me besides yourself; it is not your gift that I want, it is you.[9]

Compromise is, of course, possible. We can say we love God and go on pleasing ourselves, looking only for "sweet consolation," but this selfish attitude can never characterize the Christian. His free choice to follow Christ is an act of faith; he then chooses for

love's sake to travel happily wherever his Master
leads. Crossing desert places is not pleasant, but the
hope of reaching a more verdant valley prompts the
pilgrim to go on.

The Dark Night of Spirit

The journey to God draws us into another and
deeper kind of darkness. Now that our sensory nature
has been tested, the faculties that belong to us as spirit
and ego self must also be darkened. Darkening intellect, memory, and will leads to their perfection in
the following way: "the intellect must be perfected in
the darkness of faith, the memory in the emptiness of
hope, and the will in the nakedness and absence of
every affection."[10] Will is perfected as my love for
God expands and intensifies. I learn gradually to
forsake my self-centered attachments and surrender
wholly to him. Memory is perfected through the
purification of my trust and hope. No matter what
happens to me, no matter what has happened or will
happen, I place all my hope in my Lord and his
promise of eternal salvation, trusting as a child would
his beloved father, the workings of Holy Providence
for my good. For our purposes in this chapter, we
shall concentrate more fully on the perfection of
intellect via the darkness of faith.

As we have seen, this teaching is based on the
premise that nothing you or I can imagine or comprehend in this life can serve as a proper means for

union with God. As a matter of fact, what we do grasp
of God via the intellect can become an obstacle to
union rather than a means, if we become attached to
it. In other words, as soon as our "ideas" about God
become "idols," they block our passage to him.

> In this mortal life no supernatural knowledge or
> apprehension can serve as a proximate means for the
> high union with God through love. Everything the
> intellect can understand, the will experience, and the
> imagination picture is most unlike and dispropor-
> tioned to God, as we have said.[11]

To put it another way, however impressive our
theological credentials, however vivid our lived experience of God, we can never totally reduce to
transparency the essence of his divine majesty. Neither
explanation nor emotion can account for or contain
the mystery of God's inmost being. Neither understanding nor feeling can assure the advance
towards union. What draws us closer to him than
comprehension or imagination ever can, is abiding
with him in faith—a faith that is darkness to the
intellect, that neither depends on consolation nor
gives up because of desolation.

> . . . to be prepared for this divine union the intellect
> must be cleansed and emptied of everything relating
> to sense, divested and liberated of everything clearly
> apprehensible, inwardly pacified and silenced, and

supported by faith alone, which is the only proximate
and proportionate means to union with God.[12]

This kind of faith does not waver whether God is
experienced as near or far, as revealing or concealing,
as communicating or keeping silent. It accepts that
even the most gifted experience of God's nearness in
this life—the highest mystical moment—is still infinitely distant from him and the beatific vision of him
in the life to come.

Abiding with God in this mystery of nearness and
distance is possible only when we live in faith. Faith
opens up another realm of knowing; it lights our way
in darkness and enables us to pass beyond knowing to
the obscurity of not knowing. Paradoxically, only
when we come to this darkness do we begin to pierce
the veil that separates us from the hidden mystery of
the Divine.

> In order to draw nearer the divine ray the intellect
> must advance by unknowing rather than by the desire
> to know, and by blinding itself and remaining in
> darkness rather than by opening its eyes.[13]

It is not easy for us to abide in spiritual darkness, to
live in this tension of knowing and not knowing. The
journey homeward to divine intimacy is burdensome
for the ego and for the emotional life of man. We want
to know. We want to feel. But God leaves us in
darkness. He allows aridity. He soars above human

understanding. His wisdom exceeds the comprehending capacity of the human soul. This limitation, inherent in finite being, causes frustration. At times we feel stretched to the breaking point. But this is only one side of the story.

Although God does transcend us, he is also infinitely near us. He is with us in his Incarnate Word. He sent his own son to be our Mediator and Redeemer. Had we to rely on our own merits, this journey to intimacy would be impossible. But Jesus has entered humanity and the impossible has become possible. We are accorded all the privileges of sonship, provided we live in faithful presence to Jesus. We can place our broken self with all its burdens on our Lord. He knows from experience with his disciples how difficult it is for us to give up the comfortable niche of easy answers and warm affection. He knows that to follow him humanly, to believe in his divinity, is going to cause us unpopularity, affliction, dismay, and doubt. All we can do at such moments is to allow the mystery of his love to flow over us once again in all its impenetrability. Soon old worries, false securities, big plans, worldly popularity fall by the wayside. We accept our pilgrim status. We welcome our human limits as reminders of our need for redemption. We are aware of the danger of falling back into the falseness of an ego-centered life. But the more we grow in faith, the more we trust that God's intention is to bring us through darkness into the light.

When faith has reached its end and is shattered by the ending and breaking of this mortal life, the glory and light of the divinity, the content of faith, will at once begin to shine. [14]

All earthly suffering aims ultimately to grant us the favor of his presence. Moreover, God never tries us beyond our strength, beyond our capacity to endure. He leads us, in the darkness of not knowing, to the light of new becoming in Christ. He lets us gain in faith a few glimpses of our final goal.

Effects of Abiding in Divine Darkness

The spiritual master assures us that behind the shadows of darkness and uncertainty there beams the light of God's love and his desire to lead us home. Out of this darkness will come a new dawning of our love relationship with the Divine, a clearer sense of who we most deeply are, of where he is asking us to go.

Gifted moments of communion, once granted by God, destroy all traces of arrogance. They heighten immensely our gratitude for the Father's loving nearness in Jesus. No longer are we lost in the world as weak victims of evil; we are sons of the Father. The God we believe in is not an impersonal deity but a personal savior, a God in pursuit of man, a God who offers us a bond of intimacy that is beyond time while being wholly in it.

This mystery of intimacy is so overwhelming and so undeserved that no mind can grasp it. The only worthy response we can make to such a free gift of God is that of loving acceptance. When we accept the gift of intimacy God offers, we notice its effects on our daily situation. For one thing, we become more open to the presence of the Spirit in the persons and events that comprise our days. We are like finely tuned instruments picking up the subtle notes of the divine symphony.

Another effect of this encounter is a deeper love for and understanding of his word in Holy Scripture. We turn more frequently to Jesus as he speaks in the gospels; we make his teaching the mainstay of our decisions, appraising not only the immediate consequences but also the long range effects of what we decide to do. In the light of faith, we take into account the future as well as the present.

Our meeting with divine darkness also teaches us that human effort is ultimately insufficient to lead us closer to God. We experience in a personal way our utter dependence on his Holy Spirit to complete the journey homeward. As long as we abide with his Spirit, we need not fear losing the road. God will give us the grace we need to enter his kingdom; we in turn can express our longing in prayer and stand firm in the faith that he always responds.

Journal of the Journey

In darkness, and secure,
By the secret ladder, disguised,
—Ah, the sheer grace!—
In darkness and concealment,
My house being now all stilled;

. . . .

The "secret ladder" represents faith, because all
the rungs or articles of faith are secret to and hidden
from both the senses and the intellect. Accordingly
the soul lived in darkness, without the light of the
senses and intellect, and went out beyond every
natural and rational boundary to climb the divine
ladder of faith that leads up to and penetrates the
deep things of God.[15]

Faith is a gift. Through it God elevates me to
believe in things that exceed human understanding.
Like any gift, I can refuse to accept it, but if I do so, I
radically limit my possibilities for human and spiritual
growth. I attain what knowledge I can by means of
sense and reason, but I miss the invisible horizon—the
love divine behind all expressions of creative life.

Faith is a gift that increases my attentiveness to the
universe and the mystery of its unfolding. Faith allows
me to be friends with God, to encounter him as a
person who understands and accepts my inmost self,
who helps me at crossroad periods of my life to choose
the right path.

Faith enables me to call God by name and to seek

the name he has given me from the beginning. It tells me of things I could neither have seen nor understood by the light of intellect alone (for instance, the hand of God gently nudging me in a direction I on my own would never have discovered). Faith lets me rest in the awareness of his providential care, if I but dispose myself wholly to his will.

Faith is not wish fulfillment or the result of fear to face the abyss. It is an answer to that cry of terror in the night, to that soul-sinking feeling that life is so short, to that doubt if it is all worthwhile. Faith means looking over the brink, even falling in, but at last breathing free because he is there to sustain us. Faith is the struggle daily and hourly to rejoice in God's will, to know in some mysterious sense that I am bound to him by a bond of intimacy nothing can break. He is in me and I am in him.

Minutes tick by, years come and go. The endless cycle of rewards and disappointments, decisions and failures flows on. What lasts? I have no answer but faith. That dark gift beckons me on; it tells me I am living already what I so ardently desire.

In the midnight hour, my soul is in total darkness. Faith is my only guide as I move toward union with God. The initiative for this movement comes from him. I can do nothing to get there, save have faith that he will meet me in the darkness and illumine my way. It may be that I have to live in this darkness for a long time, much more aware of his absence than his presence. Out of these depths, I may be called to meet him more fully as he is. When I am reduced to nothing, he can at last be my all.

Such darkness is a fearful experience. Though I do not *feel* God's nearness, I still have to be grateful for his gifts. Darkness reminds me that I must love him for himself and not merely for what he gives or does.

This midnight kind of faith acknowledges that God is God and that I have to be content with what he gives. In this darkness I become more clearly aware of his light. He alone is holy. He alone is God. I am nothing. He is all.

This awareness can only be experienced by a soul that has cooperated with grace to uproot all traces of self love. St. John says that this uprooting comes to pass in the souls God desires to raise to new heights of union. What if he chooses me, then what? Am I willing to be purified of all self love? Can I endure the loneliness of the midnight hour? Am I willing to go through the grievous suffering of God's apparent absence, and, at the same time, to thank him for allowing this suffering to come upon me? Do I believe that he will give me the strength I need to respond?

St. John reminds me to be confident. God's fidelity to me never wavers. If I simply step toward him, he rushes out to greet me and take me home. This homecoming, above all, is what I am longing for. Many obstacles are strewn on the path but none defeat Christ's promise of divine union and transformation in God through love.

* * *

CLOSING PRAYER

Truly your ways, my God, are beyond what I can
know.
From reason's view, everything seems reversed.
Your seeming distance is true nearness,
The prayer I find so poor,
Is the one you find most pleasing.
Reason leads me far,
But faith alone can cross the last abyss.

Let me lay before your altar
My weakness and my trust.
Teach me to wait upon your will
While being where I am.
Let me give you a free hand
To guide me where you must.
Lead me through this night
To a union that transcends all knowing.
Let me love you for yourself alone.
Then I shall be ready to go home,
Attentive to you for your sake and not my own.

CHAPTER TWO

Awakening From Illusion

Spiritual reading can be an avenue to spiritual awakening. It can serve as a watchman directing the soul back to the right road, warning us when we are about to take an unnecessary detour, providing a flashlight when we find ourselves going off on an illusory tangent. The power of the word can help us to pierce through the veils of illusion woven by vital needs and ego controls in isolation from the spirit. These screens—pleasure bound or power hungry— shield the soul from the reality that it is primarily God, not world centered.

If nothing else, spiritual reading inclines us to slow down, to reflect, to become more thoughtful about our situation instead of acting on fantasy or reacting impulsively. It helps us to refind our center when, because of weakness or pride, we lose the path to God and become spiritually decentered. Abiding with the word can serve as a kind of lever to put us back on center as followers of Christ and not some vital or ego substitute.

When we do slowed-down meditative reading on a regular basis, the wisdom of the masters can awaken us from needs and desires that detract us from our journey homeward, provided we open our ears inwardly to the truth of their message. To do so, we have to establish in ourselves the proper disposition, namely, an openness to the word that is at the same time a willingness to listen and be transformed by what we hear.

Reading in the spiritual sense aims to clarify our inner vision. *Vacate et videte quoniam ego sum Deus* (Ps. 45:11). St. John quotes this phrase in *The Ascent* and translates it as: "Learn to be empty of all things— interiorly and exteriorly—and you will behold that I am God."[1] Contrary to my being empty for God, I am often full of worldly concerns. I awaken in the morning thinking not of him but of the myriad things I have to do. How can I be empty and see my God if I am so full of myself? Instead of focusing on things as ends in themselves, I need to focus more sharply on the Transcendent. What I see is the same but now things take on a deeper meaning. They become pointers to the beyond rather than obstacles to transcendence.

Something similar happens when I put my glasses on. The scene that was blurred before now emerges in full detail. Without glasses I could see the cottage tucked amidst tall pines, the boat bobbing on the icy blue lake, but not sharply. I could make out some features, but precise details blurred into one another. With glasses on, I behold what is there in all its God-given beauty.

This putting on of one's glasses also provides a good image of what happens in spiritual reading. With the right lenses on, the "blur" of confusion begins to disappear and we see in more detail what the text is pointing to. As spiritual readers, we seek contact with the sacred word as a guide to inner awakening. What makes this brief sojourn on earth a journey homeward to God? What blocks our moving onward? We know from our reading that illusion is a problem rooted in the human condition. The pride of man since the fall poses a major obstacle to spiritual awakening. We live in falsehood when we regard our individual ego as the only or central reality. We idolize ourselves instead of the Sacred. Though it may seem an easy order to let go of the ego as absolute, this too is a false conclusion. It is a difficult and life long task to break through the wall of pride the ego prefers to retain; it is utterly impossible to do so without God's grace.

The journey homeward will come quickly to a halt unless we awaken with the help of grace to the illusion of making our isolated "I" the only reality that counts. The ego is not meant to be an object of worship but an "incarnating bridge" spanning the distance between the inner self or spirit and the world or situation in which we find ourselves.

In several of his writings, Adrian van Kaam explains that the ego is meant to be a servant of the spirit self, not its own idol. Neither, therefore, should the ego be destroyed or weakened. We need to behold ourselves and all creation against the divine horizon. We are limited and finite; God alone is eternal—the source and sustaining ground of all that is. In this awakened condition, we let go of the ego's deceptive clutch; we become flexible and receptive to the invitations of the spirit self. We welcome our place in creation. We break through the illusion of a man-centered existence and become a willing medium through which the Eternal Word incarnates itself.[2]

Obstacles to Awakening

Certain obstacles in the self can block this graced possibility of our becoming channels through which the Divine Word can flow. One of these is the loss of right balance. In attempting to describe the fall of man, we often point out that man "lost his balance." He upset the right relationship that existed between himself and God. He tried to be not like God but God. We too live in this unbalanced condition, ever marring the delicate lines of relation between creature and Creator. This condition affects all levels of our being, sensual and spiritual. For instance, our ears lack right balance from a spiritual view when rather than hearing the words of the Lord, we prefer to catch every new phrase that comes along. Our ears are like megaphones, picking up the latest gossip as preferable to listening to God's voice. Our eyes lack right balance when they light upon whatever curiosity craves. They are not inner-directed eyes that behold the Face of God but outer-directed eyes, immodestly grabbing onto whatever worldly sight attracts them. Our speaking does not flow out of personal reflection on God's word; it merely echoes what everyone else is saying. Given this condition, how do we regain the right balance between sense and spirit? St. John offers this counsel:

> For example, if you are offered the satisfaction of hearing things that have no relation to the service and glory of God, do not desire this pleasure or the hearing of these things.
>
> When you have an opportunity for the gratification of looking upon objects that will not help you come any closer to God, do not desire this gratification of sight.
>
> And if in speaking there is a similar opportunity, act in the same way.
>
> And so on with all the senses insofar as you can duly avoid this pleasure. If you cannot escape the experience of this satisfaction, it will be sufficient to have no desire for it.
>
> By this method you should endeavor, then to leave the senses as though in darkness, mortified, and empty of pleasure. With such vigilance you will gain a great deal in a short time. [3]

The spiritual master identifies the source of our difficulty as displaced desire. Hearing, seeing, and speaking are God-given capacities that ought to lead us closer to him, but because of our fallen nature, we tend to be led only by what satisfies us. Therefore, in order not to live in illusion, we need to be vigilant; we need to discipline our desires in the direction of God and his glory, not our gratification only.

If our senses cause us to live in illusion due to lack of vigilance, so too can our spiritual faculties of memory, intellect and will be off balance. Memory that neglects to remember God and hope in his saving power tends to imprison us in the past. We may become morbidly introspective, reviewing in endless succession all our faults instead of remembering God's forgiveness.[4] Intellect untempered by faith demands tangible proof of God's presence. We lose ourselves in images and arguments that can never pierce the hidden mystery of his being. Will becomes distorted when it arouses in us affections for self and others that belong rightly to God. He alone can be the object of our adoration. We are to love him with our whole mind and heart and soul and to let this love spill over in charity toward our neighbor. When any or all of these faculties are thrown off balance, we risk losing the way of hope, faith, and love God wants us to follow.

Another obstacle to spiritual awakening involves what St. John calls the "appetites." Appetites are desires directed to worldly goods as ultimate. They bind us to created things as if they could fulfill our longing for the eternal. Due to this excessive attachment, we become like blind men living in the illusion that what will satisfy us is one or the other temporal person or thing. St. John wants to awaken us from this illusion by showing us that the "only appetite God permits and wants in His dwelling place is the desire for the perfect fulfillment of His law and the carrying of His cross."[5] He wants to arm us with a whole set of reasons why we should mortify these misdirected appetites, the main one being that they deprive us of God's Spirit.

To help us understand what happens, he refers to the Gospel of Matthew, which reads: "It is not fair to take the children's food and throw it to the house dogs" (Mt. 15:27) and to another passage, "Do not give dogs what is holy . . . " (Mt. 7:6). The children of God are all those who ready themselves for the pure reception of God's Spirit through the denial of their desires to possess creatures as sources of ultimate fulfillment. The dogs are all those who desire to find in creatures the fulfillment only God can provide.

> Our lesson here is that all creatures are like crumbs which have fallen from God's table; and that they who go about feeding upon creatures are rightly designated as dogs, and are deprived of the children's bread, because they refuse to rise from the crumbs of creatures to the uncreated Spirit of their Father. This is precisely why they wander about hungry as dogs. For the crumbs serve more to whet their appetite than to satisfy their hunger.[6]

By not tempering our attachments to creatures, we deny ourselves access as children of God to the un-created fullness of his Spirit. His Spirit wants to find entry into our souls, but God can hardly fill us if we are already full of other desires. He seems to prefer an empty heart in which to make his dwelling place.

St. John gives five other reasons for redirecting our desires. If we allow them to "run wild," they will *weary, torment, darken, defile,* and *weaken* the soul.[7]

Misdirected desires are wearisome basically because they resemble restless little children who are im-possible to please. Give them one thing and they want another. Give them an inch and they take a mile. They are always whining for this or that and never seem satisfied. St. John suggests other comparisons of which the two following are most vivid:

> The man seeking the satisfaction of his desires grows tired, because he is like a famished person who opens his mouth to satisfy himself with air, only to find that instead of being filled his mouth drys up more since air is not his proper food.[8]
>
> Just as a lover is wearied and depressed when on a longed-for day his opportunity is frustrated, so is a man wearied and tired by all his appetites and their fulfillment, because the fulfillment only causes more hunger and emptiness. An appetite, as they say, is like a fire that blazes up when wood is thrown on it, but necessarily dies out when the wood is consumed.[9]

Torment and affliction are the second kind of damage excessive desires cause. The greater the appetite for some vain pleasure, the more intense the torment it occasions. Whether the desire is fulfilled or frustrated, it still torments. Take the Don Juan type. He is tormented if his desire for pleasure eludes him; he is equally tormented when the seduction succeeds and he finds himself feeling empty. Concupiscence only fires up our thirst and makes it worse. The Spirit of God refreshes and brings us peace.

Thirdly, untempered desires that take up all our time and thought by seeking fulfillment of them, blind or "darken" us on many levels. They impede our intellect from enjoying the light of natural reason, to say nothing of supernatural wisdom. Due to this blinding of intellect, St. John says, the will becomes weak and the memory dull. The intellect darkened by desires is incapable of receiving the illumination of God's wisdom; the will, thus weakened, cannot embrace his pure love; the memory can no longer maintain the serenity of God's image upon it. Every time selfish desires take over, we become like men with poor eyesight being led by the blind. And ". . . if one blind man leads another, both will fall into a pit." St. John minces no words on this point:

As the tilling of soil is necessary for its fruitfulness—
untilled soil produces only weeds—mortification of

the appetites is a requisite for man's spiritual fruitfulness. I venture to say that without this mortification all a man does for the sake of advancement in perfection, and in knowledge of God and of himself, is no more profitable than seed sown on uncultivated ground. Accordingly, darkness and coarseness will always be with a soul until its appetites are extinguished. The appetites are like a cataract on the eye or specks of dust in it; until removed they obstruct   vision.[10]

Our predicament is like that of Solomon's. For all his wisdom, he was unable to restrain rushing after his own desires. Failure to deny them gradually darkened his intellect so that finally the powerful light of God's wisdom went out.

According to St. John, any appetite, even one that is slightly disordered, stains and defiles the soul. Basically this defilement occurs because inordinate attachment makes a soul destined for God bound to what is not God. Just as strokes of soot ruin a perfect portrait, so disordered desires besmerch the soul, which is in itself "a perfect and extremely beautiful image of God." Until the life of desire is purified, the soul is incapable of conformity with God in a union of likeness. The disordered soul may possess in its natural being the perfection God bestowed when creating it, but it is called to much more: to a union so lovely that any marring of it by displaced desire is self-destructive according to St. John.

Lastly, appetites weaken a soul and make it lukewarm in the practice of virtue. They sap the strength needed to devote ourselves to God. They drain off energy that could be channeled into his work. Because the force of desire is divided across many desires, it becomes weaker than if it were fixed on one object, namely, the Divine. It follows, then, that if the desire of the will extends to something other than God and the life of virtue pleasing to him, it grows weaker as time goes on. The soul that is not recollected in one longing alone, namely, the desire for God, is bound to be less zealous in the practice of virtue. Unless we strive to moderate excessive desires, the result will be a drying up of our love for God.

St. John adds that he is referring here as elsewhere to the "voluntary appetites"—from the most serious which involve mortal sin to the least grave that concern venial sin and imperfection. We must be liberated of all of these, however slight, to arrive at perfect union. Natural longings are impossible to eradicate in this life; we may experience these desires in the sensitive part of our nature and yet not will them when their fulfillment would be at odds with God's will for us. Even while a person is experiencing an intense union of will in the prayer of quiet, these desires can disrupt the sensory part. The soul should then not pay the least attention to them. To be freed from every appetite means in effect not to give the consent of our will knowingly to an imperfection. As

St. John stresses in his famous imagery of the solitary bird, any habitual imperfection and our attachment to it can impede union:

> It makes little difference whether a bird is tied by a thin thread or by a cord. For even if tied by thread, the bird will be prevented from taking off just as surely as if it were tied by cord—that is, it will be impeded from flight as long as it does not break the thread. Admittedly the thread is easier to rend, but no matter how easily this may be done, the bird will not fly away without first doing so. This is the lot of a man who is attached to something; no matter how much virtue he has he will not reach the freedom of the divine union. [11]

Signs of Awakening from Illusion

Unless with God's grace we can begin to unmask and overcome our misguided desires, we cannot hope to journey home. Once we begin to awaken, we see how necessary it is to refer all things to God, to recognize that he is the author of all good, to accept ourselves as sinful creatures in need of redemption. Of the many signs of spiritual awakening we could consider, three stand out. These are taken from the counsel of a wise friend and contemporary of St. John's, Mother Teresa of Avila. Being asked by her sisters to map out for them a way of perfection, she responded with her book of the same title. She had no intention of making the way of awakening overly complex for these simple sisters; so she told them that, besides praying without ceasing, there were three points to remember: Love each other, that is, practice fraternal charity. Be detached. Be humble.[12]

Love. A first sign of awakening from illusion involves the letting go of self-centered tendencies that separate me from my neighbor and build barriers of envy and prejudice between us. Others are placed in the "enemy camp" if they become more successful than I. The tendency to label blinds me to the unique self-worth of each person God allows to cross my path. When I live in the illusion of self-sufficiency, I feel proud of being able to make it on my own. The feeling of not needing anyone deceives me into thinking I don't even need God.

Awakening from this illusory state of total independence may happen in many ways. For instance, all appears to be going well. I'm up and about—healthy as can be! Then, without warning, I fall suddenly ill. That bubble of joyous and vigorous self-sufficiency bursts. Now I know how much I depend on others. Their charity toward me in time of need makes me realize how lonely I've been in my prison of self-love. I realize that life is empty unless one reaches out in love to others and to the Divine Other. This wakeful moment may lead me to change my life style. Guarded defensiveness gives way to fraternal kindness. Suspicion is tempered by trust. Now I can feel compassion for others' needs. I wonder what I can do with Christ's help to relieve their burden.

The grace of this conversion from "me-love" to "mutual-love" is the gift of our Lord. He is the model of self-giving St. Teresa asks her sisters to imitate. He will teach them how to have equal love for one another so that no love becomes exclusive, save their love for God. He will help them overcome their vain prejudices and open up to the bond of communion that makes all of us members of his Mystical Body. The sweetness of love we experience in union with him overflows graciously into the effective love through which we serve others.[13]

The more we practice fraternal charity, the less it matters to us if our love is returned in kind and degree. Reciprocal affection is fine, but it is not a necessary condition to go on loving. Here we follow Christ's way. He loved to give and kept on giving, even when his kindness was not returned. The highest form of love, according to St. Teresa, is "love without any degree whatsoever of self-interest; all that this soul wishes and desires is to see the soul [it loves] enriched with blessings from Heaven."[14] This "wakeful love" is a far cry from the "wearisome desire" St. John warned us against. It "is a similitude and copy of that which was borne for us by the good Lover, Jesus."[15]

Detachment. Misplaced desires blind me to the truth that only God is ultimate fulfillment, but I can awaken to this truth through detachment. Detachment is St. Teresa's second sign that we are living as wide-awake Christians, who see that created goods are destined to point us toward the Creator. Any exclusive attachment to them cuts us off from what we really seek; not the gifts of God but the Giver who offers them to us.

St. Teresa suggests as a test of detachment that her sisters assess how they relate to their relatives. Does being with them disrupt their spirit because they tend to get overly involved with family matters? Can they listen politely to their troubles, while maintaining inner tranquillity, or do they get embroiled in this or that detail?

Unwise attachment can often make a mountain out of a molehill in family matters. I recall in this regard that one of my aunts wrote a letter to a niece in which she gave her version of a particular incident that had occurred between them. In this case it had to do with buying a gift that turned out to be inappropriate. The buying, however, was done in good faith and the letter was written to explain the aunt's version of what happened. A remark was made in the letter to the effect that even though her niece didn't like the gift, her aunt "still loved her anyway." The niece in turn passed that remark on to her sister who made a great "do do" about it. "What does she mean she still loves you anyway! Didn't she love you before?" It took many calls and letters after that for the aunt to explain the real attitude expressed in her original letter. When this story was related to me, as an objective outsider, I was asked such questions as, "What should I do? Should I apologize? Should I try to explain that I really didn't mean that? I meant it as a joke. Will they understand? Maybe they'll think I'm just defending myself," and on and on.

Never before had St. Teresa's seemingly harsh words to her sisters about relating to relatives made such sense: "Oh, if we religious understood what harm we get from having so much to do with our relatives, how we should shun them! I do not see what pleasure they can give us, or how, quite apart from *the harm they do us as touching* our obligations to God, they can bring us any peace or tranquillity."[16] She advises her sisters to commend their relatives to God, for that is only right, but for the rest to keep them out of their minds as much as possible. Since their desires are naturally attached to kinsfolk more than to other people, this attachment sticks to them most closely and is the hardest to get rid of. For this reason, she implies, they must heed Christ's words, "I tell you solemnly, there is no one who has left house, wife, brothers, parents or children for the sake of the kingdom of God who will not be given repayment many times over in this present time and, in the world to come, eternal life."[17] These words convince St. Teresa that she and her sisters must find everything in him, and so for his sake forget everything. Of course, she does not mean to condemn a wise and loving concern for family and relatives even if we are called to a life of contemplation.

Attachment to petty matters may seem appropriate in the "short run", but this view is an illusion. Real help in human relations may only be forthcoming when we forget about our solutions and complaints and give the matter over to God. Clinging to the immediate severs us from the wider reality of the situation as God views it. Before we know it, we are trapped again by self-will. Being creatures of this earth, we are prone to become exclusively attached to our point of view. Detachment happens whenever we step aside from a self-imposed solution to listen to God's word. It happens when some material good we thought would make us totally happy inevitably disappoints us. These experiences, and ones like them, alert us to the fact that we must let nothing deprive us of the holy freedom of spirit our souls seek "in order to soar to their Maker unburdened by the leaden weight of the earth."[18]

Humility. A third sign of awakening from illusion involves humility, which St. Teresa calls an inseparable sister of detachment. For her, humility means simply walking in the truth of who I am—freed from the deception of sovereignty, accepting with joy my creaturehood, delivered from the entanglements of pride prompted by the devil.[19] The humble person knows his limits and possibilities. He neither pampers his vital self nor imposes upon it impossible penances. St. Teresa, like all wise spiritual masters, is suspicious of feats of asceticism in which pride hides itself under the cloak of humility. She is also suspicious of the scrupulous person who fancies herself humble because she points unceasingly to all her faults. Such a person overlooks the fact that the center of her attention is still self—not God.

Continual moanings are not signs of humility for St. Teresa. True interior mortification has to do with an attitude of inner poverty and the surrender of one's will to God. Anyone who has a "martyr complex" risks again being trapped by pride posing as humility. This snare also catches the person who pays too much attention to her honor, who is overly sensitive to blame or overly dependent on praise. The weakness of human nature comes as no shock to St. Teresa. She realizes that the gift of knowing myself is not gained without a life-long struggle to overcome the ingenious wiles of self-deception.

As aids to self-knowledge, St. Teresa recommends being satisfied to be the least of God's servants; imitating the great humility of Mary; recognizing our own faults in a gentle fashion and hesitating to point out the faults of others; finding our self-worth in the service of God not in our feelings of ego-gratification; rejoicing in the liberation such renunciation brings

For St. Teresa, a sure sign of awakening from the deception of pride involves keeping silent when we find ourselves unjustly condemned.[20] Recalling the way our Lord stood before his accusers, she says it is better to be silent than to raise our voices in self-defense—save, of course, in those few cases where hiding the truth might cause offence or scandal. That picture of Jesus taking human abuse so humbly because he saw his responsibility before the Father truly inspired her. We can do no better than to imitate our Lord, who did not blame his enemies but forgave their blindness.

The path of humility is the way to atoneness with the Father. On this road I recognize the misery and weakness of the human condition, resulting from original sin. I know that I will never be entirely free from its effects in this life. One side of growing in humility thus entails standing in the truth with a knowledge of and love for myself as I really am. The other side is to recognize, as St. Teresa did, the transcendent goodness of God, who in his Incarnate Word showed an overflowing superabundant love for each of his fallen creatures—good, though weak; prone to deception, but still infinitely precious and worthy of salvation.

The author of *The Cloud of Unknowing,* in teaching his disciple about the nature of humility, stresses, as does St. Teresa, that the blinding light of God's love illumines all human darkness. It is the key to spiritual awakening: "Before such goodness and love nature trembles, sages stammer like fools, and the saints and angels are blinded with glory."[21]

Journal of the Journey

> The soul's center is God. When it has reached God with all the capacity of its being and the strength of its operation and inclination, it will have attained to its final and deepest center in God, it will know, love and enjoy God with all its might.[22]

+

Love is what unites me with God as my center. Self-deception and excessive ego defenses keep me off center. Love loses its intensity when the desire for anything other than God's will fills my soul. Take the example of excessively desiring some concrete wish to come true in the near future. I struggle to diminish the vehemence of this desire, which begins to dominate my life, but it comes back again and again. Each time it lessens my capacity to accept in equanimity the will of God no matter what happens.

St. John has said that it is the nature of one who has self-centered desires to be ever discontented and dissatisfied. The more I think about this, the more I realize how right he is. When I vehemently want something to happen, I argue pro and con, I feel unhappy, I want to control the future. I begin to fret and fume about it. I pray over it. I tell God that I want to leave the future up to him, but my actions show I don't really mean it. I keep going back to what I desire so violently, not really able to let go. Without this letting go, no peace of mind is possible. Anxiety and tension build. I tend to want my way, no matter what, instead of waiting to see what God's way is for me.

When I look back over my life, the Lord may grace me with seeing much evidence of his generosity toward me. In his protective care and sustaining love, he has fulfilled many desires of mine. Those he has redirected have been, in retrospect, for my best good. But am I content or is there always a new desire to burden myself with? Instead of simply living day by day in trustful presence to his will, I conjure up another burning wish.

Perhaps God expects this restless asking from such a needy creature. Requesting only favors that conform to his will is one kind of prayer. Another is to simply be in his presence, loving him for himself and not for what he gives me. This simple declaration of love brings my spirit to rest. Desires quiet down. This quieting occasions relief from fatigue and needless worry. Past, present, and future are placed in God's hands and life regains its peace.

Desire has to be diminished if I am to refind the simplicity of faith, if nearness to God is to become my main goal. My consciousness of persons, things, and events must be placed in service of the spirit center of my being where the Holy Spirit reigns. Then my enlightened consciousness becomes a purified channel through which God's grace can flow.

I know my Lord, that true spirituality is born of your Spirit alone. Help me to continually prepare the way for your presence. Never let me forget that your grace prompts me to this action and carries it to conclusion. Without you, I can do nothing.

This process of prayer and purification goes on as long as I journey to my goal. Without it I could make no progress on the road to perfection, no more than the seed planted on untilled ground can grow. Fertile ground for divine wisdom consists in the graced mortification of all self-centered desires, of putting myself utterly as the disposal of my Lord.

* * *

CLOSING PRAYER

Lord, awaken me from the sleep of desire
That makes me oblivious to my heart's longing.
Lift the illusion that hides the truth
That giving up self is really gaining.
Allow my soul to soar homeward with ease,
Freed from entanglements of mere worldly concern.

Strengthen me, Lord, for the mighty task
Of removing obstacles that block your grace.
Lead my soul into a silence so deep
That only your voice reaches my ears.
Gather my wounded being to yourself
By detaching my soul from earthly desires
That tend to exclude remembrance of you.

In this life-long endeavor to diminish desire
Help me endure the dryness I feel.
As I follow you to desert places,
Give me to drink of living water,
Refresh me with your endless graces.

Without your grace to give me strength,
I might despair of even trying.
What you measure is not my success
But the tireless effort to struggle onward.

I cannot promise to never resist you,
For ego is not easily tempered.
I can promise that despite my resistance
My love will last with tenacious persistence.
Though mistakes will be made
And detours taken,
Trusting your wisdom

I need not feel forsaken.
The night is dark, the journey long,
But your mercy is there to lead me on.

CHAPTER THREE

Spirit of Prayer

When we pray, we affirm the bond of intimacy that exists between ourselves and God. Prayer draws us out of our narrow egos and towards the Divine Other. Everyone who longs for the Divine and seeks to transform his will has to follow the path of prayer.

In *Maxims on Love,* St. John says: "Seek in reading and you will find in meditation; knock in prayer and it will be opened to you in contemplation."[1] In this short sentence he establishes an essential relationship between four practices of spiritual living: reading, meditation, prayer, and contemplation.

A predecessor of St. John's—one Guigo II, known also as Guigo the Angelic (+ 1188), ninth prior of the monastery of the Grand Chartreuse—wrote a letter later entitled *Steps of the Cloistered Life* to share with one of his brothers some thoughts on the spiritual formation of monks.[2] In the letter he envisions a ladder stretching from earth to the heavens along these same four steps: *lectio, meditatio, oratio,* and *contemplatio.* Giugo probes the meaning of these steps through an investigation of their properties and functions.

Lectio involves the initial attention paid by the

person to the careful investigation of Scripture and spiritual masters. The function of reading is "to seek." Guigo says it provides solid food for the soul and is the foundation that sends one on to meditation. It is the practice of beginners. Without meditation, reading remains arid. *Meditatio* implies studious action of the mind as it investigates the knowledge of hidden truth under the impetus of one's reason. Meditation, as it were, masticates and breaks up the food. It uncovers the inner reality of the word and prepares the way for desiring God's will. It is an action belonging to the proficient. Without reading, meditation is erroneous; without prayer, it is fruitless. *Oratio* moves the person from the mind into the heart. Through it one savors the fruit of the word. Prayer impels the person to the desirable treasure hidden in reading and uncovered partially by meditation. It belongs to the devoted and leads the soul naturally into contemplation, described by Guigo as the elevation of the mind in suspension to God. Contemplation consists in the sweetness which rejoices and refreshes; it attains the desirable treasure and belongs to the blessed. Clearly reading, thinking, praying, and contemplating are necessary steps on the road to union. Each practice may vary in degree of intensity but together they lead the soul to God.

Prayer of Quiet

Turning now from the relationship between these four spiritual practices, we can focus on another main movement in the life of prayer: that from discursive meditation to the prayer of quiet, sometimes called "acquired or active contemplation" to distinguish it from prayer of union, "infused or passive contemplation."[3] The same movement is described by St. Teresa of Avila in her autobiography where she presents her famous analogy of the "Four Waters."[4]

Briefly, St. Teresa distinguishes four ways of irrigating a garden. The garden stands for the soul and the water signifies ways of prayer that lead the soul into an ever more intimate union with the Lord of the garden. The first way to water the garden is by taking water from a well, an action that requires of us a good deal of labor. To this action St. Teresa compares the way of meditation or "active recollection." It is the way of beginners who are learning to keep their senses recollected, to apply the faculties of memory, intellect, and will to Father, Son, and Holy Spirit, to the mysteries of faith.

The second way of watering is by use of a water wheel and buckets, when the water is drawn up by a windlass. This method is less laborious and gives more water. To it St. Teresa compares the prayer of quiet or "passive recollection." Here the soul begins to recollect itself in a way it could not experience by its own exertions. Memory and intellect are less active now; the will without knowing how becomes more and more lovingly attentive to God; it wants to make its abode in him—loving without understanding, remaining calmly with him in peace and solitude devoid of self interest.

The third way to irrigate the garden is by planting it near a stream or brook which naturally saturates the ground and makes the gardener's labor much less than before. In St. Teresa's description, this third water stands for the prayer of simple union—in mystical life, the stage of spiritual courtship and espousal. Here the Bridegroom comes to the Bride in a union incomparably sweeter than anything the soul has previously experienced. Its faculties seem to be asleep; specific acts of memory, intellect, and will cease as the soul is lifted into the arms of God. These visits, though brief in duration, give the soul what it could never acquire by its own labor. The experience is one of death to self mingled with ineffable joy.

The fourth, and by far the best way of watering, happens when it rains. Now the Lord waters the garden with no labor of ours. The rain comes from heaven to fill and saturate the whole of the garden with an abundance of living water. This fourth water refers to the prayer of perfect union—in mystical life to spiritual marriage. The Bride is overjoyed by this privilege, uplifted in a blissful union she can never understand. The soul almost faints completely away; it can apprehend nothing with the senses which only hinder its joy; all outward strength vanishes while strength of spirit increases. What God has granted the Bride is the gift of no longer living in herself but being wholly at one with him.

Keeping St. Teresa's analogy in mind, we can now return to St. John's description of how we move from meditation to prayer of quiet. He depicts meditation as the work of two faculties: imagination and phantasy. Through imagination we can carry our meditation along from point to point; through phantasy we can form in our mind material images and figures to support the scene from the life of Christ or the scriptural passage we are meditating upon. Especially in the beginning stages of the life of prayer these faculties play an active role and are most instrumental in training the mind to concentrate on God and on the great generosity he has shown to mankind through the mysteries of Incarnation and Redemption. But, as we advance in prayer and reach out toward deeper intimacy with the Divine, we have to begin the slow process of emptying our minds of ideas and images, of forms and figures, fashioned by these senses. The reason for doing this is because our imagination cannot fashion or imagine anything beyond what has been experienced through the senses—that is, what our eyes have seen, our ears have heard, and so on. Now, as St. John sees it, created things are unproportioned to God's being. Therefore, all imaginings fashioned out of similarities to them are for that very reason incapable of serving as a proximate means toward union with God. In the life of prayer, we must start out by climbing the steps of considerations, forms, and concepts but—if we want to arrive at union with the "Supreme Repose and Good in this life," we must eventually leave these behind and abide in the calm of interior quietude. Grace invites us to this next stage of prayer, but we may not heed this invitation:

> Many spiritual persons, after having exercised themselves in approaching God through images, forms, and meditations suitable for beginners, err greatly if they do not determine, dare, or know how to detach themselves from these palpable methods. For God then wishes to lead them to more spiritual, interior, and invisible graces by removing the gratification derived from discursive meditation.[5]

The invitation to move beyond meditation, once it has been initiated by grace, may persist. Hard as we strive to meditate, we draw little or no satisfaction from it. What used to be a gratifying spiritual exercise, now leaves us feeling arid, fatigued, and restless of soul. Try as we might to make particular acts via the use of memory, intellect and will, we are drawn to one general act of quiet, loving attentiveness to God. Rather than trying to acquire spiritual nourishment through the labor of imagination, we are more and more drawn to the repose of inner quietude, to being filled with the peace and refreshment of God. One seems moved less by excessive efforts or studied reasonings and more by what God is effecting in him. Because this process initiated in us by grace may confuse many spiritual persons and their directors, St. John gives some signs for recognizing when it is time to pass from the stage of discursive meditation to that of active contemplation or the prayer of quiet. From the onset he insists that these signs have to be operative together; one without the other is not sufficient evidence of a genuine call to prayer of quiet. In the journey to God, it is necessary not to abandon imaginative meditation until the time is right, for this style of prayer is a remote means of union with God for beginners. Moreover, even those more proficient in prayer (to say nothing of the "perfect" who experience still higher graces of infused contemplation) will at times return to the practice of meditation and work with the natural faculties. This need continues until one acquires the habit of contemplation in a certain perfect degree.

For example, along with the high graces of mystical union St. Teresa received, she returned again and again to loving meditation on the humanity of Jesus. At times she experienced total absorption in the Trinity, the suspension of all her faculties, even the utter transcendent bliss of spiritual espousal and marriage but she never lost her devotion to the earthly Jesus in Nazareth, the Holy Family, the saints. She taught her sisters to become proficient in mental prayer and the other stages via meditation on the "Our Father."[6]

Keeping in mind the importance of vocal prayer

and meditation, we can explore the three signs St. John gives as an aid to recognizing the opportune time to discontinue meditation. The first involves the simple realization that I cannot meditate in a discursive fashion nor receive the same satisfaction as I did before. The outcome of fixing my senses upon subjects that were formerly most satisfying is now dryness. Where before I could meditate in a disciplined way on an event from the Gospel—for instance, Jesus' encounter with the Samaritan woman—thinking about what our Lord said and how the woman responded, now I find it difficult to concentrate on such details. Try as I might to understand what was going on between Jesus and the woman and to apply the deeper meaning of this meeting to my life, I feel somewhat dry and distracted. This feeling might be due to a lazy mind or a momentary melancholy; that is why I must watch for the second sign.

Secondly, I have to be distinctly aware of a disinclination to fix my imagination or sense faculties upon particular objects, whether these be exterior or interior. The workings of imagination may come and go but I have no inclination to affix them purposely upon extraneous things. This is not to say, following the above example, that I lose interest in the Samaritan woman and the encounter Jesus had with her. Something prevents me, however, from staying with this particular meeting in its concrete details, from imaginatively being in that place at that time. Consider another example of the same. Formerly, I might have been able to feel truly inspired to worship the suffering Jesus by meditating on the crucifix. My outer vision and inner imagination could remain attentive to that sacred object and all that it signified. Meditating on it might occasion in me a profound moment of communion. For the time being, however, I experience an inability to meditate in this manner. St. John cautions, on the one hand, that this inability to dwell on anything in particular may only signify a lack of diligence; on the other hand, it may be a sign that I want my prayer to be one of quiet presence to the Divine Persons, one of being with God more than thinking about him. St. John insists these two signs appear together; namely, that we can no longer meditate in the way we did before and that we can no longer fix our imagination on particular objects.

The third and surest sign is that I like to "remain alone in loving awareness of God, without particular considerations, in interior peace and quiet and repose, and without the acts and exercises (at least discursive, those in which one progresses from point to point) of the intellect, memory, and will . . . "[7] I want to be so quiet that I even cease striving to increase my understanding of him, perhaps because I have begun to discover that no matter how much I know about God, I am miles away from his true mystery. I do not desire precise knowledge of him; all I want is to love him. I want to remain with him in the loving awareness of faith, whether I understand what is happening to me or not.

Again, St. John writes, I must observe within myself all three signs *together*. Otherwise I risk living in spiritual illusion. Say I were to experience the first without the second. This inability to imagine and meditate could derive from dissipation of the life of prayer, lack of diligence, or sheer laziness. What if the first and second signs are present but not the third? I feel incapable of making discursive meditation; I am disinclined to think about subjects extraneous to God, but I am not experiencing this intense desire to remain alone in loving awareness of him. The cause, then, could be "melancholia" or "some other kind of humor in the heart or brain capable of producing a certain stupefaction and suspension of the sense faculties."[8] I could mistake this abnormality for a call to quietude.

The grace of the prayer of quiet is initially easily overlooked because at the beginning of this state of prayer the loving knowledge being granted the soul is almost unnoticeable. Ordinarily, its movement into the soul is extremely subtle and delicate, "almost imperceptible." Then, too, one who is habituated to the exercise of meditation, which is wholly sensible, hardly perceives this new "insensible, purely spiritual experience." This is especially the case when he does not permit himself any quietude because he fails to understand what is happening; all he can think of doing is to seek after more stimulating sensory experience. The interior peace God is extending may be abundant, but the person (or his director) allows no room for its experience and enjoyment. Despite these difficulties, St. John holds to the necessity of these three signs if one is to continue to journey on the road of Spirit and spiritual life.

> . . . the more habituated he becomes to this calm, the deeper his experience of the general, loving knowledge of God will grow. This knowledge is more enjoyable than all other things, because without the soul's labor it affords peace, rest, savor, and delight.[9]

In the prayer of quiet, I may feel as if nothing is happening at all, but the more I grow accustomed to this calm, the deeper my loving awareness of God may become. While I am doing less in terms of my own effort and initiative, I am coming to know and love God more. I feel attuned in faith to his initiative. I appreciate anew the spiritual nourishment I receive from the regular sacramental and liturgical life of the Church. Far from falling into a kind of quietism, such prayer leads me to the fullness of participation, for now my life of action is nourished and transformed by my life of presence to the Divine.

Prayer of Quiet and Purgation

In Book I of *The Dark Night,* St. John describes the purifying process grace is working in the soul when the

prayer of quiet is granted.[10] God allows certain
sufferings to occur in order to draw us into a higher
degree of divine love. He desires to liberate us from
the exercises of the senses and of discursive meditation
(exercises which are good but inadequate for the goal
of union) and lead us into the exercise of spirit, in
which he is the principle agent. St. John's experience
has been that God more and more takes over after we
have practiced for some time the way of virtue and
persevered in meditation and prayer. God works in
the following mysterious manner with souls about to
be drawn closer into his love:

> Consequently, it is at the time they are going about
> their spiritual exercises with delight and satisfaction,
> when in their opinion the sun of divine favor is shining
> most brightly on them, that God darkens all this light
> and closes the door and spring of the sweet spiritual
> water they were tasting as often and as long as they
> desired . . . God now leaves them in such darkness
> that they do not know which way to turn in their
> discursive imaginings; they cannot advance a step in
> meditation, as they used to, now that the interior
> sensory faculties are engulfed in this night. He leaves
> them in such dryness that they not only fail to receive
> satisfaction and pleasure from their spiritual exercises
> and works, as they formerly did, but also find these
> exercises distasteful and bitter. As I said, when God
> sees that they have grown a little, He weans them from
> the sweet breast so that they might be strengthened,
> lays aside their swaddling bands, and puts them down

from His arms that they may grow accustomed to walking by themselves. This change is a surprise to them because everything seems to be functioning in reverse.[11]

When things begin to function in reverse, one naturally feels afraid. Perhaps I have gone astray. Am I deceiving myself into thinking that God is giving me these gifts? Am I praying to please myself or to praise God? I may suffer from the fear that God has abandoned me altogether when I can no longer experience his presence as vividly as before. My inclination then is to work harder at meditation, to fill up the silence with holy thoughts.

To clarify the causes for this fear and confusion, St. John again gives three signs, based on his experience, by which I can discern if I am truly being granted the grace to tread the path of sensory purgation. St. John first points out that the origin of these aridities may not be the sensory night and purgation; they may be caused by sin, imperfection, weakness, lukewarmness, some bodily indisposition. If, however, the following three signs are found together, the dryness experienced almost surely is the result of purgation by grace rather than being caused by one or the other of the defects just mentioned.

The first sign has to do with the fact that I do not derive satisfaction or consolation from the things of God; in nothing created do I find sweetness or delight.

The Bride in *The Spiritual Canticle* feels this aridity when she cries:

> Where have You hidden,
> Beloved, and left me moaning?
> You fled like the stag
> After wounding me;
> I went out calling You, and You were gone.[12]

St. John explains the phrase "left me moaning" to mean that since the Bride loves nothing outside of the Bridegroom, she finds no rest or relief in anything; anything less than God leaves her feeling dry and discontented. She has learned that satisfaction of heart is not to be found in the possession of things but in being stripped of them all in poverty of spirit.

> The soul, then, bears this moan within herself, in her enamored heart. For there where love wounds is the moan rising from the wound, and it ever cries out of the feeling of His absence; especially when the soul, after the taste of some sweet and delightful communication of the Bridegroom, suffers His absence and is left alone and dry.[13]

Because of his visits, the withdrawals of the Bridegroom are felt with keener sorrow. Still, to return to *The Dark Night,* this lack of satisfaction in earthly or heavenly things might be the product of some indisposition or lingering imperfection. Thus the second sign or condition must accompany the first.

Ordinarily the memory turns to God in great solicitude and painful care to appraise whether or not I have been serving him faithfully or turning back. Is this distaste for the things of God due to aversion or laxity in spiritual practices? A lukewarm person probably would not even ask such a question so already this inward solicitude is a sign that something more is going on. I feel deprived of every satisfaction and am concerned *only* about serving God. If melancholy were the entire cause of these inner movements, everything would end in disgust; but I feel more and more desirous of being his servant. The sensory part of the soul may be cast down, but the spirit is "ready and strong."

> The reason for this dryness is that God transfers His goods and strength from sense to spirit. Since the sensory part of the soul is incapable of the goods of spirit, it remains deprived, dry, and empty, and thus, while the spirit is tasting, the flesh tastes nothing at all and becomes weak in its work. But the spirit through this nourishment grows stronger and more alert, and becomes more solicitous than before about not failing God.[14]

St. John compares what is happening within the soul to what happened when God led the children of Israel from Egypt into the desert.[15] At first their palate longed to return to the "fleshmeats and onions" they had eaten in Egypt. They were unaccustomed to the "delicate sweetness of angelic manna." It took a long period of purgation to transfer their tastes from sense to spirit. Similarly, the food God is offering at the beginning of contemplation may taste dry to the senses but it is providing strength and nourishment to the spirit. God's way at this time is to purify the interior faculties by leading them to their proper spiritual end. He leaves the intellect without support so I can grow in faith; he diminishes satisfaction in the will so I can grow in purity of heart; he takes away remembrance of earthly goods from the memory so I can fall back upon him in hope. My own efforts at this time are of little avail because God is doing the work. In fact my efforts may only prove to be an obstacle to the interior peace and good God is bringing the spirit via dryness of sense.

> Since this peace is something spiritual and delicate, its fruit is quiet, delicate, solitary, satisfying, and peaceful, and far removed from all these other gratifications of beginners, which are very palpable and sensory. For this is the peace that David says God speaks in the soul in order to make it spiritual. (Ps. 84:9).[16]

The third sign for discerning this purgation follows from the first two: namely, the powerlessness, despite my efforts, to meditate and make use of the imagination as was my prior custom. This powerlessness is due to the fact that God does not communicate himself through the senses as he did before. Neither discursive analysis nor the synthesis of ideas suffices to bring him near. Now that he has become the principal agent, he chooses to communicate himself "through pure spirit by an act of simple contemplation, in which there is no discursive succession of thought."[17] Therefore, one can conclude that the dissatisfaction of the faculties is not due to laziness or any indisposition. For if that were the case, I could return to my former exercises with ease once the indisposition passed away.

But such is not the case; the powerlessness to meditate continues, either totally or partially. It is up to God to determine the degree of intensity of the next stage of prayer. St. John claims that God "does not bring to contemplation all those who purposely exercise themselves in the way of the spirit, nor even half."[18] He best knows why. Many reach prayer of quiet but the higher stages of spiritual espousal and marriage are rarer privileges that it is God's sole prerogative to decree. For some the flame of God's love flickers with a steady warm glow; for others it flares up in heat and intensity; for still others it becomes a raging fire so intense that the soul is literally consumed in God.

On the Way with Prayer

From these considerations, we can see how important it is for the pilgrim to grow in the spirit of prayer. To pray does not imply having already reached a certain perfection. We can go to God with empty hands, signifying our lack of power. We can go to God without having to know the "right words." It is in praying that we will find the words we are looking for and when words cease, it is enough to pray in silence—to believe that the Holy Spirit prays in us, expressing our plea in a way that could never be put into words.[19]

God himself said to us that we are to watch and pray. "You should be awake, and praying not to be put to the test."[20] "Be happy at all times; pray constantly; and for all things give thanks to God, because this is what God expects you to do in Christ Jesus."[21] This commandment is a personal word addressed to each of us. It is an imperative, a demand. We are free to choose or reject it, but we cannot alter the fact that the commandment is there.

The object of prayer is to bind us to God in childlike obedience. The God to whom we pray is supreme Good. Once we meet him in prayer, we know in a way we cannot explain that he is present in us at all times, lovingly letting us be and directing our lives. We want to discipline ourselves so that at each moment we are in tune with the will of God and happy to accept our dependence on him in body and soul.

Not everyone prays in the same way. There are many levels and degrees of prayer. However, if there is one spirit common to the person who prays, it is the spirit of humility. The praying self is humble, a faithful servant of the Lord, rejoicing in the many gifts he has received, grateful beyond measure that God in his goodness has reached out and redeemed him in his nothingness.

This touch of God makes it impossible for us to keep him in the background. We want him to be with us more consciously each day: with us in the decisions we make, and the errors we repent; with us in the present and when planning our future; with us in the ups and downs of daily life.

Spiritual deepening through prayer is a hidden process. Though many times on the journey homeward, we do not know what is happening to us, we give God the leeway to lead; we pray that he will prepare in us an ever more fertile ground that grace can act upon. So great is the power of the Divine Word to change and transform our lives, so overwhelming is the goodness of God, that no complex phrase can grasp it. At times nothing suffices but a silent leap of love that proclaims: You alone are holy! You alone are Lord!

Journal of the Journey

When the spiritual person cannot meditate, he should learn to remain in God's presence with a loving attention and a tranquil intellect, even though he seems to himself to be idle. For little by little and very soon the divine calm and peace with a wondrous, sublime knowledge of God, enveloped in divine love, will be infused into his soul. He should not interfere with forms or discursive meditations and imaginings. Otherwise his soul will be disquieted and drawn out of its peaceful contentment to distaste and repugnance. And if, as we said, scruples about his inactivity arise, he should remember that pacification of soul (making it calm and peaceful, inactive and desireless) is no small accomplishment. This, indeed, is what our Lord asks of us through David: *Vacate et videte quoniam ego sum Deus* (Ps. 45:11). This would be like saying: Learn to be empty of all things—interiorly and exteriorly—and you will behold that I am God.[22]

+

In meditation there is often a dialogue going on between myself and God about one or the other event in my life and its connection with him and his life. For example, at moments when I perceive my own suffering as growing in intensity, or when I look around and see the marks of suffering on the faces of fellow men, I like to meditate on Jesus' agony in the garden.[23] What he must have endured as he looked back and ahead to all the ways men would suffer because they betrayed him! Seeing him, my heart is moved to pity. I feel badly when I deliberately offend him—say by an act of uncharitableness to another—because I realize that this act added to his suffering.

Many passages in the Gospel provide food for meditation: the days of Jesus in the desert, the beatitudes, his last words on the cross. In this kind of prayer, my mind is at work, along with imagination and feeling.

In the prayer of quiet, all these words and images

give way to the silent surge of love. I do not want to speak. I want simply to listen to the silence that surrounds the suffering Christ, to be present to his power of presence in the core of my self, to gaze lovingly upon him and feel incapable of uttering one word.

Though I am still active in this prayer, it may happen, when I have been led this far by God, that he will go a step further and take me totally out of myself and into him. At such rare and gifted moments, the Bridegroom comes after the Bride, who loses herself in his presence.

In the prayer of quiet, there is thus no desire to fix my senses upon any particular inner or outer object. Just to gaze lovingly upon God is enough. During this prayer, the reasoning process gives way to the simple and loving intuition of eternal truth. The soul is prepared for this prayer by frequent meditation and discursive acts in which the mysteries of faith and the ways of God are reflected upon. But in quiet prayer itself, the soul is like one to whom the water has been brought; he drinks peacefully, without labor, and is no longer forced to draw water through the aqueducts of past meditations and forms and figures.

It is God who is the principal agent of this prayer. He fills the soul with blessed tranquillity and brings it to that childlike, open, and trusting love that is the sign of my cooperation with his grace. This prayer leaves the soul in forgetfulness of self; it pierces the heavens and transcends time. Such lofty heights may be reached only for brief moments, but they are gifts whose value is never forgotten, wells from which we continue to draw living water in the darkest night.

On these occasions, I may feel as if nothing is going on. I may be tempted to do something, but it is best to simply live this period of quiet as it comes, softly calling upon Jesus' name or praising him from my heart while not making any extraordinary effort to put into words what is wordless. The prayer of quiet is essentially silent.

I grow silent when I see myself in God's light and realize that I am nothing. For all my good will, I am incapable of freeing myself from base modes of acting; I am wholly dependent on the purity and fidelity of God's love, manifested most dramatically in Christ's redemptive act. I cannot rise up by my efforts alone. I need redemption. The miles I have to cover are not covered by me but by the Lord coming to meet me with his gift of mercy. If I desire him truly, he does not tarry. He comes eagerly to greet me.

God's grace, his friendship, is not far away or long in coming. I can love him now. Now he is coming to meet me. I need only to turn toward him in trustful prayer. He is there, waiting for me to awaken from the sleep of illusion, to leave the prison of egoism. Tranquillity, equanimity, Jesus' gift of peace can be mine once I discover the secret presence of God within. As the vast horizon of his mystery opens up, I can declare with St. John:

Mine are the heavens and mine is the earth. Mine are the nations, the just are mine, and mine the sinners. The angels are mine, and the Mother of God, and all things are mine; and God Himself is mine and for me, because Christ is mine and all for me.[24]

The master tells me that all is mine by virtue of God's union with me. It is not necessary to seek for fulfillment in outside things. Look within and find the answer, he seems to say. Recognize the eternal sea in which you are already swimming. All the ways you have regarded yourself—as mean and insignificant, as worthy or unworthy of the crumbs that fall to you from the Father's table—must be silenced. Forget this counting and measuring. Forget this calculative mood where grace is concerned. God's goodness is boundless. Go forth in freedom and glory in his glory. Glory in the reality of being man and being redeemed. Rejoice because God is living in you. Hide yourself in him. Worship and silently adore his presence that fills the heavens and the earth. You need not do spectacular things nor receive extraordinary favors to find what your heart desires. What you desire is hidden within if you will rub your eyes clear of the dust of intervening desires and desire the one thing necessary: his presence in you, his will for your life. Then you will have all you desire.

* * *

CLOSING PRAYER

Lord, lead me to silence
And the prayer of inner quiet
That I may follow your light to life eternal.
The fullness and oneness I seek
Can never be found
Amidst the fragments of earthly life.
I seek instead the undivided splendor of your
Kingdom.

I need silence to keep my life in perspective,
To hear of its passing and know that I am mortal.
I need silence to heal me from the hurt of speech,
To hear in worldly sounds the Voice most pure.

I feel dispersed among dry leaves of endless prattle,
Lost in words that touch only surface meanings.
Silence plunges me into inner depths
Where night descends,
Handmaiden of your mystery.

In the night of sense deprivation
Your silence stills all words.
You are the measure against which I feel infinitely
small.
Your silence speaks to me of the mystery of being.
You spoke in eternal silence
The Word who was your Son.
The silence of loving attentiveness
Is the language you hear best.

Wisdom is to keep silent
And wait upon your Word.
What is prayer but to be quiet before you?
To still desire,

To give my petitioning tongue a rest.

In silence, with you as my center,
We meet as friends.
Defenses drop,
There is nothing to hide,
No one to impress.
My secret self is known in the silence by you, Father,
Who from silence called me forth
And to whom, in silence, I shall one day return.

CHAPTER FOUR

Sin and Forgiveness

It is impossible for us as Christians to speak of sin without at the same time speaking of forgiveness. I once heard a homily given by a priest who had spent many years in Africa as a missionary. He told the story of how he, with all his training and expertise, learned the meaning of his faith anew through the eyes of these pagan people. What he wanted to tell us about was not what he had given to them but what they had given to him.

Of all the doctrines and teachings of the faith he introduced them to, the one that caused both him and them the most difficulty was the teaching concerning sin. The more he preached to them about sin, the more anxious and guilt-ridden these simple people became. He said that gradually, although with much pain, they were able to accept the fact of their own sinfulness, but what they bewailed again and again was the great sorrow they felt for their ancestors. What had happened to their forefathers since they did not know what sinners they were?

The more the priest tried to quell their fears, the more frightened the people became. He felt that something was wrong with this whole approach. So he decided to read the Gospel again carefully to see if he could discover his mistake, trying to discern also in the Acts of the Apostles what Peter and Paul did in their missionary work. Before long, the light began to dawn that really these early missionaries did not focus mainly on sin; they told potential converts about the Christ who came to forgive sins, the Savior because of whom their sins were pardoned and through whose power they were reunited with the Father. Christian faith was not to be lived out of fear due to sin but out of love due to forgiveness. The reaction of these simple, loving people to the doctrine of sin awakened him to the wider horizon of forgiveness in which all teaching on sin must be placed.

It was easier then for him to teach the people. He began in his homilies to focus first on Christ's forgiveness. They loved this approach. Wrongdoing was not a thing to avoid because of fear of punishment but because it would hurt the Lord who loved them so much. Their whole motivation to be good changed from one of fear to one of love. Through them the priest discovered that without this horizon of forgiveness the sinner almost commits a double sin— the sin itself and the sin of introspectively focusing on himself sinning instead of humbly presenting himself before God, confident that by Christ's action he has been "fore-given." This realization is, of course, no excuse for sinning. The people understood that. The Christian is to avoid sin, but he must never forget that

God is there—as was the father for the prodigal son—to welcome him back when he falls away.

Christ's forgiving of us ought to be our precedent for forgiving others. To imitate our Lord in his forgiveness, we must learn also to forgive ourselves, for how can we help to heal the hurt between man and man that makes for a sick society unless we are able to forgive one another as well as ourselves.

As receivers of Christ's redeeming grace, we know that our sins have been forgiven. This is a deep truth of our faith. As one Preface of the Holy Mass puts it, in love he created us, in justice he condemned us, in mercy he redeemed us. As we shift the focus from self as sinning to God as redeeming and forgiving, we turn the direction of our spiritual life from sin to forgiveness, from sorrow to thanksgiving, from suffering to joy, from isolation to brotherhood. This shift is necessary for the journey homeward. We must never forget the severity of sin in all of its forms—what it does to us interiorly and what it does to our relationship with God—but neither must we forget the undeserved gift of forgiveness.

Ways of Turning from God

Sin is not a substance, like a thing or an object within us that renders us evil; sin is rather a swerving of the will, a turning away from God in preference for our own power, pride, avarice, and lust. In turning away from God, we do not necessarily separate ourselves totally from him for all time to come. Every turning away is potentially a being-called-back by his forgiveness and redeeming love.

Sin can be compared to loss of sight. In turning our gaze from God, a kind of blindness overtakes us. We live in obscurity and ignorance. We experience the tension St. Paul tells of in Romans 7: 15: "I cannot understand my own behavior. I fail to carry out the things I want to do, and I find myself doing the very things I hate." Sin can thus be regarded as a certain defectability of choice due to the fact of original sin. Though created good, we have this propensity to choose evil. Our decisions can become disordered in some way.

Especially as beginners on the spiritual road, we are likely to fall into several common imperfections. St. John takes as his key to these the capital sins.[1] If we can see ourselves in what he writes, we may be able to recognize these vices as blocking the way to union, avoid them as much as possible and ask for God's forgiveness when we fail.

Pride. Beginners have to be on guard that their first fervor and diligence in spiritual exercises does not lead to a secret pride, a complacency with all that *I* have accomplished. What might be some signs of this offense? One is a vain desire (because I like to be the focus of attention) to speak of spiritual matters when I am sure others are listening. I experience a newly found expertise to instruct others and dislike being told what to do. I look around, as the Pharisees did, and secretly condemn others who seem less devout than they should be. Before long the Tempter leads me to turn virtue into vice. Others become the object of detraction whenever the occasion arises. I see the splinter in their eye but remain oblivious to the plank in my own.[2] I put the blame for a director's disapproval on his lack of understanding or holiness and quickly seek out a spiritual adviser more to my liking—someone who will congratulate me and be impressed by my deeds. Those who don't affirm me I flee from or feel hostile towards. I love to receive praise and seek it out but dislike passing it on to others.

Other signs of spiritual pride begin to plague me. I make big resolutions but accomplish little. I badly need the approval of others so I begin to make movements, sighs, and other public ceremonies that attract their notice. The author of *The Cloud of Unknowing* noticed the same tendency and pointed it out to his disciple:

The spiritual and physical comportment of those involved in any sort of pseudo-contemplation is apt to appear very eccentric, whereas God's friends always bear themselves with simple grace. Anyone noticing these deluded folk at prayer might see strange things indeed! If their eyes are open, they are apt to be staring blankly like a madman or peering like one who saw the devil, and well they might, for he is not

far off. Sometimes their eyes look like the eyes of
wounded sheep near death. Some will let their heads
droop to one side, as if a worm were in their ears.
Others, like ghosts, utter shrill, piping sounds that
are supposed to pass for speech. They are usually
hypocrites. Some whine and whimper in their desire
and eagerness to be heard. This is the approach of
heretics and those clever and conceited folk who argue
against the truth. [3]

St. John says the beginner may carry this phony
behavior into the confessional and only relate sins in a
favorable light. Penance becomes an occasion to
excuse rather than to accuse myself. Good deeds are
made to appear greater than they are and faults are
either glossed over or ignored, minimized or made
into mountains. The motive for asking forgiveness is
more personal peace than reconciliation with Christ.

Opposite patterns of spiritual growth are observable
in souls advancing in perfection. Some signs of
progress are these: I place little importance on my own
deeds and don't take much satisfaction in them. My
typical inclination is to believe that everyone else is far
better than I. If I envy them, it is with a "holy envy"
because I would like to emulate their service to God.
Becoming truly humble shows up in an increasing
fervor to do good deeds; the gratification received in
the doing only directs me to be more aware of my debt
to God and my inadequacy to serve him. Loving
solicitude for God preoccupies me so much I am

unable to believe it when I receive the praises of others. I consider my deeds insignificant, so why should others call attention to them? My desire to be taught is so strong I would never think of teaching when not called upon or commanded. I am eager to obey those ordained to instruct me, to speak openly to a spiritual director of my faults and sins, to seek direction from a person more likely to admonish than to admire. When I do fall into imperfections, I suffer this fall with humility and docility of spirit, with loving fear of God and hope of his forgiveness. St. John says God grants these humble ones his graces, together with other virtues; he leads them into the dark night to purify their souls of any lingering imperfections and make them advance in virtue.

Avarice. This vice shows up in the discontent I feel with whatever spirit God gives me. I become unhappy and peevish due to lack of consolation. As a result I greedily collect more spiritual things like counsels, maxims, and books; I become attached to ornate images, rosaries, relics, and crosses; I even collect mortifications and penances—all to the detriment of detachment and interior poverty.

> Since true devotion comes from the heart and looks only to the truth and substance represented by spiritual objects, and since everything else is imperfect attachment and possessiveness, any appetite for these things must be uprooted if some degree of perfection is to be reached. [4]

Again the author of *The Cloud*, though writing before St. John's time, agrees with his thoughts. He compares the avaricious initiate to a "greedy greyhound suffering from starvation."[5]

> Yet unfortunately, these people believe that the excitement they feel is the fire of love kindled in their breasts by the Holy Spirit. From this deception and the like spring evils of every kind, much hypocrisy, heresy, and error. For this sort of pseudo-experience brings with it the false knowledge of the fiend's school just as an authentic experience brings with it understanding of the truth taught by God.[6]

Spiritual avarice has to be quelled at the outset of one's journey; otherwise my eyes become fixed on the consolations of God rather than on the God of consolation. Souls making a good beginning generously give all to God and neighbor and cling no more to spiritual benefits than to temporal goods. Their eyes are fastened on the way of interior perfection—on pleasing God—and not on themselves. These souls, too, will receive the grace of "God's divine cure"—the passive purgation of the dark night that aims to heal imperfections no effort of our own could remedy.

Lust. In discussing this imperfection (which generally accompanies complacency of the will), St. John notes that impure movements are at times experienced in the sensory part of the soul, even when the spirit is deep in prayer or receiving the sacrament

of penance or the Eucharist. These feelings arise
without my consent from any of three causes. They
may proceed from the pleasure human nature finds in
spiritual exercises, which gratify both the spiritual
and sensory part of the soul according to each one's
own nature and properties. Early in the spiritual life,
sensory gratification may predominate over spiritual
renewal and satisfaction in God, but this imbalance
can be corrected through the purgation of the dark
night.

A second origin of these sensual rebellions,
movements, and acts is the devil. St. John identifies
one of his tactics as that of bringing disquiet and
disturbance upon the soul at prayer or when trying to
pray. He deliberately incites impure feelings in the
sensory part of the self. These feelings only become
harmful when I pay attention to them, when through
fear I grow slack in prayer or, worst of all, when I give
up prayer entirely. This is exactly why the devil stirs
up these feelings when I am praying rather than
working: his intent is that I abandon prayer due to the
fact that these feelings and impure thoughts come up
more often and more violently then than at any other
time. The problem is compounded if one suffers from
"melancholia." His trial may reach such a point that
he thinks the devil definitely has access to him without
his being able to prevent it. In such a case, one may
not be freed of these impure thoughts and feelings
until he is cured of this sickness, and the dark night of

God's purifying and healing grace flows in upon his soul.

St. John suggests astutely that the third origin of these feelings is none other than the fear of them. That fear springs up at the sudden remembrance of these thoughts and produces in turn impure feelings without one's being at fault. Due to a certain constitutional make-up, a person may immediately translate gratification received from the Spirit or from prayer into "a lust which so inebriates them and caresses their senses that they become as it were engulfed in the delight and satisfaction of that vice . . . "[7] The same thing happens when they are angry or agitated; any change stirs up their blood in a lustful manner.

St. John identifies other behavioral patterns that are by-products of spiritual lust, for example, a showing off in conversation or work depending on who is present. One may also acquire a liking for other individuals which arises from lust rather than from the Spirit. I can tell the difference between genuine spiritual friendship and a relation of lustful origin when remembrance of that affection awakens not love of God but remorse of conscience. An affection is truly spiritual "if the love of God is remembered as often as the affection is remembered, or if the affection gives the soul a desire for God—if by growing in one the soul grows also in the other."[8]

Love born of spiritual lust has contrary effects: the

soul grows cold in the love of God and due to the recollection of that other love forgets him. What should happen is that the soul cools the inordinate affection and comes to love God more and the other in God. When the dark night enters the soul, it puts all these loves in reasonable order, strengthening and purifying the love of God and taking away the imperfections of lust.

St. Teresa of Avila comes to the same conclusion when she gives advice about spiritual friendship in *The Way of Perfection*: "When a friendship has for its object the service of His Majesty, it at once becomes clear that the will is devoid of passion and indeed is helping to conquer other passions."[9] Passion in this context refers to illicit attachment between religious persons whose exclusive love for one another gains ascendancy over their love for God. This kind of false friendship may gratify the friends, but little by little it deprives them of the strength of will they need to center themselves wholly in the love of God.

Anger. The desire for spiritual gratification seems to be the root cause of many imperfections of anger. When that first delight procured in spiritual exercises passes, I may be left devoid of any spiritual savor. Because things that formerly pleased me have become tasteless, I may grow peevish while going about my work. The least thing that goes wrong flares me up. I may become unbearable to live with—just like a petulant child when nourishment is suddenly withdrawn. St. John feels that the best and only ultimate cure for this fault is the dryness and further distress of the dark night.

There is another kind of spiritual anger he notices, especially in community. It happens when, due to an indiscreet zeal on my part, I become angry over the sins of others; I reprove them in anger rather than in gentle admonition, thereby setting myself up as a master of virtue. I may turn my anger destructively back upon myself, growing angry at my imperfections and railing at myself with unhumble impatience, as if I could and should become a saint in a day! The angrier I grow at my faults, instead of humbly asking for forgiveness, the more grandiose my resolutions become. When I break these, as is bound to happen, I grow doubly angry. I simply don't have the patience to wait until God gives me what I need "when He so desires." Since my attitude is contrary to spiritual meekness, it, too, can only be remedied by the purgation of the dark night.

Gluttony. St. John says that few, if any, beginners escape totally the many imperfections associated with spiritual gluttony. These, too, arise from the delight beginners find in spiritual exercises. The natural consequence of this delight is to desire more: to "strive more for spiritual savor than for spiritual purity and discretion" despite the fact that "it is this purity and discretion which God looks for and finds acceptable throughout a soul's entire spiritual journey."[10]

A person may be so attracted by the satisfaction he receives in spiritual exercises that he begins to kill himself off with penances, to weaken himself by fasts, to even perform these mortifications when commanded by his director not to do so. But corporal penance without obedience, reason, and discretion is of no merit in the spiritual life. As the author of *The Cloud* says:

> For the love of God, then, be careful and do not imprudently strain yourself in this work. Rely more on joyful enthusiasm than on sheer brute force. For the more joyfully you work, the more humble and spiritual your contemplation becomes, whereas when you morbidly drive yourself, the fruits will be gross and unnatural. So be careful. Surely anyone who presumes to approach this lofty mountain of contemplative prayer through sheer brute force will be driven off with stones. Stones as you know are hard, dry things that hurt terribly when they strike. Certainly morbid constraint will also hurt your health, for it is lacking the dew of grace and therefore completely dry. Besides it will do great harm to your foolish mind, leading it to flounder in diabolical illusions. So I say again, avoid all unnatural compulsion and learn to love joyfully with a sweet and gentle disposition of body and soul.[11]

What motivates me is not pleasing God by these penances but an appetite for the pleasure I gain in them. Any time I do not tread the path of obedience, I risk becoming spiritually gluttonous and proud. The devil may stir up this gluttony by impelling me to add, change, or modify what I've been commanded to do. Obedience becomes more and more repugnant. I derive satisfaction only when doing what I feel inclined to do. I may even try to force permission for such indiscreet practices from my spiritual director, convinced that by gratifying myself I am serving and satisfying God. If I do not get what I want, I become sad and testy like a spoiled child. I spend so much time trying to get some feeling and satisfaction from spiritual exercises (such as receiving Holy Communion) that I neglect to humbly praise and revere God dwelling within me. If sensory benefits are not forthcoming, I think I have failed God. What I have failed to see is that he may deliberately withdraw sensory delight to foster an increase of faith. This desire to feel and taste God, as if he were comprehensible and accessible, is a serious imperfection, according to St. John, because it involves impurity of faith and is, therefore, opposed to God's way.

Spiritual gluttony causes one to search for spiritual consolation, to crave sweetness, to do all kinds of extra mortifications and meditations—anything but following the common way of the daily cross. "A soul given up to pleasure naturally feels aversion toward the bitterness of self-denial."[12] In the night of spiritual aridity, the imperfections of gluttony may give way to spiritual sobriety and temperance, helping the soul to become aware that "the perfection and value of his works does not depend upon their number, nor the satisfaction found in them, but upon knowing how to practice self-denial in them."[13]

Envy and Sloth. In regard to envy, I may feel sad about the spiritual good of others and grieve when I note that my neighbor is ahead of me on the road to perfection. It saddens me to hear others praised; my usual tactic at such times is to contradict the praise in some subtle way, to undo these compliments as much as possible. I grow annoyed when praises are not directed my way because I long for preference in everything. Such imperfections are contrary to charity, which rejoices in goodness, and contrary to "holy envy," which saddens me because I do not have the virtues of others and makes me happy to see others ahead of me in the service of God.

In regard to sloth, I may become weary of spiritual exercises and flee from them when they cease to yield spiritual satisfaction. I become bored with prayer or go to it begrudgingly. Due to sloth I subordinate the way of perfection to the pleasure and delight of my own will. I feel averse to adapting my will to God's and begin to think that if *I* feel satisfied *with me* so too must God. Sloth also makes me shy away from doing anything unpleasant. I grow lax in fortitude and the labor perfection demands. I am scandalized by the cross and run from anything that is rough.

For envy and sloth, for all these ways of turning

from God, the turn toward him happens by his introducing the soul into the dryness and interior darkness of the purgative way. We shall explore the particular afflictions and benefits of this night in the following chapter. For now we want to focus on the gift of God's forgiveness and the demand it makes upon us.

Gift and Challenge of Forgiveness

After the fall into sin, man was obliged to repair the breach between himself and God, but on his own merits he was incapable of doing so. Therefore God took the expiation of sin upon himself in the person of Jesus. By his suffering and death, Jesus rendered to the Father vicarious atonement for the sins of men. The redemptive action of Jesus not only granted remission from sin; it also bestowed the grace that leads to heaven. Christ's sacrificial death on Calvary was at once the perfect atonement for our sins and the meritorious cause of our justification before God. Whatever grace we receive comes to us, therefore, through the merits of Jesus.

Through Baptism the guilt of sin is removed and we are reinstated in God's friendship. All punishment due to sin is also mercifully forgiven. What remains is the infirmity of our fallen nature—the concupiscence or unreasoning appetite that can lead to sin. But as long as we do not consent to wrong desires or impulses, we continue to gain merit in the sight of God. The sufferings we experience because of our unruly passions have within them the seed of virtue. When we bear these trials with patient resignation and prayers for divine assistance, we make progress on the road to spiritual perfection.

Though our sins are forgiven due to the merits of Jesus and the grace of Baptism, full remission of sins committed after Baptism, together with restoration of friendship with God, requires a sincere conversion of heart and amends made for the injustice committed against his goodness. Such restoration is accomplished through confession and repentance for sin, making up for the wrong done, and freely accepting the punishments demanded by an all-wise and loving Lord. This action is meant to impress upon us the folly and gravity of sin and its harmful consequences to mankind.

Forgiveness is God's gift to us, but it also implies a demand in the practical and social order of life. We are called to imitate the Father's forgiveness of his disobedient children by forgiving as we have been forgiven. Jesus taught this lesson in the Lord's Prayer:

> Give us today our daily bread.
> And forgive our debts,
> as we have forgiven those who are in debt to us. [14]

He repeated the same teaching many times in the New Testament, for instance, when he told the story of the lost sheep; ". . . I tell you, there will be more rejoicing in heaven over one repentant sinner than over ninety-nine virtuous men who have no need of repentance."[15] Or when he answered Peter's question about how many times to forgive his brother if he wrongs him: "As often as seven times?" Jesus answered, "Not seven, I tell you, but seventy-seven times."[16] Indeed the Father will deal with us without pity unless we take pity on our brothers and forgive them from our hearts.

Jesus teaches this lesson in the parable of the unforgiving debtor. We all know the story of the king who decided to settle his accounts with his servants.[17] One of them, who owed him ten thousand talents, had no means of paying; so the king ordered that he should be sold, along with his wife and children and all his possessions, to pay the debt. Now the servant threw himself at his master's feet and begged him for some time to find the means of payment. Jesus tells how the master felt sorry for him and decided to let him go, cancelling the debt. Jesus is, of course, comparing this earthly act of forgiveness to the mercy outpoured by his heavenly Father. The expectation is that men must do the same for one another. But, sadly, such is not the case, as we find out when Jesus continues the story.

Soon after the servant had been forgiven by the master, he met a fellow servant who owed him a small sum of money. He grabbed him by the throat and began to beat him mercilessly, demanding that he pay what he owed. The fellow servant was in the same position as he was when he went before the king— unable to pay and asking for time to meet the debt. But the unforgiving servant took no pity on his friend's plight; he promptly threw him in prison until he could pay. This action so deeply distressed the other servants that they went to the king and reported these events to him. The master immediately sent for the wicked servant and reprimanded him severely. He reminded him of how his debt had been cancelled when he appealed to the king, but he obviously paid no attention to this act of mercy. When the chance came to take pity on a fellow servant—as the king had pitied him—he stood in unforgiving judgment. The master's anger this time could not be assuaged; he handed the servant over to the torturers until he could pay all his debt. "And that," Jesus says, "is how my heavenly Father will deal with you unless you each forgive your brother from your heart."[18]

Forgiveness has to be from our hearts; that is, an act of our whole person. It cannot be merely a mental or emotional gesture. Jesus' act of forgiveness was, of course, totally expressed; he expressed it not only with words but with his whole life. Mindful of him, my feeling, thinking, willing, and remembering self has to be involved in the act of forgiveness; I cannot keep the forgiveness I feel inside myself. I have to try to express it in some way, however embarrassing or painful this experience may be.

Involved in forgiveness, besides expression, is a letting go of the displeasure I feel toward the other for what he has done to me. This is the "forget-aspect" of forgiveness. Why is it so hard for me to do that? Perhaps the difficulty lies in the instinct I feel to preserve *my* reputation, *my* property, *my* ideas. This instinct for ego-preservation is powerful; that is why it can prevent me from truly forgiving the other; that is, not only saying, "I forgive you," but letting go of the displeasure I feel.

Contrary to forgiveness is my tendency to make the other the *object* of my forgiveness. I do not really regard him as a person, but simply as a bad object whom I, in my great generosity, can forgive. Similarly, I can refuse forgiveness or prevent it from happening within me if I identify a person with his actions only, as if the whole of him can be reduced to what he did or did not do. If that happens, it might be impossible for me to forgive him. I see only his weakness and ignore his virtues and good will; I merely identify him with the wrong he did. I can also fail in true forgiveness when I falsely forgive the other for the sake of preserving and promoting my ideal self-image of the forgiving one. Such condescension is not forgiveness. It can really frustrate the other person, making him feel guilty and uncomfortably beholden to me.

Genuine forgiveness, as the parable of the unforgiving debtor so well portrays, emerges from the conviction that I and the other are already "fore-given." Jesus is always forgiving us. We have a small part to play after all. The other has already been forgiven by Jesus in his act of ransoming us from sin. If I can remember that, then it may not require such a great effort on my part to forgive. My forgiveness is only a follow up of what Jesus has already done.

In my deepest self, I desire, as Jesus taught, to restore peaceful union and communion between myself and my brothers; I want to diminish the unpleasant feelings of tension and dissension that have grown between us. For the sake of reestablishing inner peace and harmony, I try at least to bridge the gaps between us by keeping my sense of humor. I note that the person who refuses to forgive quickly loses his sense of humor; he is usually unable to take hurt with a grain of salt. Unlike this person, I have no illusions about the human condition; I do not expect perfection. I accept in myself and the other not only our divine but our demonic tendencies as well. Both of us are inclined to evil. Neither of us can be his own savior.

To forgive and keep on forgiving, we must believe in our hearts that there is really no limit to this gift, no end to its challenge. If this awareness becomes the ever present background and support of our life, we may gain an efficacious means to ward off impatience, intolerance, and injustice; a strong barrier against the danger of becoming embittered, gloomy, or broken when in the course of life disappointments and misunderstandings come. Once we believe that the Infinite Spirit does understand and forgive us, we can grant the same forgiveness to others and to ourselves. Healed by this merciful approach, which calls to mind the Father's forgiveness of the prodigal son, we and our fellow pilgrims can journey home.

Journal of the Journey

You were never better off than now, because you were never so humble nor so submissive, nor considered yourself and all worldly things to be so small, nor did you know that you were so evil, nor did you serve God so purely and so disinterestedly as now, nor do you follow after the imperfections of your own will and interests as perhaps you were accustomed to do. What is it you desire? What kind of life or method of procedure do you paint for yourself in this life? What do you think serving God involves other than avoiding evil, keeping His commandments, and being occupied with the things of God as best as we can? When this is had, what need is there of other apprehensions or other lights and satisfactions from this source or that. In these there is hardly ever a lack of stumbling blocks and dangers for the soul, which by its understanding and appetites is deceived and charmed; and its own faculties cause it to err. And thus it is a great favor from God when He darkens them and impoverishes the soul in such a way that it cannot err with them. And if one does not err in this, what need is there in order to be right other than to walk along the level road of the law of God and of the Church and live only in dark and true faith and certain hope and complete charity, expecting all our blessings in heaven, living here below like pilgrims, the poor, the exiled, orphans, the thirsty, without a road and without anything, hoping for everything in heaven?[19]

+

As I walk this pilgrim's path to God, bearing the burden of sin and error, I feel sustained by his forgiveness. He listens to my longing for his presence. He teaches me to follow the "level road" of his law in obedience and love. He asks me to make him the center of my life by letting go of self-centered desires and the sins they give rise to: pride, avarice, envy, sloth. As long as lack of peace torments my soul because desires rule, I cannot be liberated by obedience to my Lord. Only when I am occupied with the things of God can he lead me out of the land of darkness, exile, and thirst and into the land of "true faith and certain hope and complete charity." Guided by his law, drawn on by his word, I can become a true disciple, extending to others the liberating offer of forgiveness.

Even as I write these words, I realize how far I am from fulfilling this commission. My thoughts and acts are still divided from God, yet I need not grow discouraged. The words of the spiritual master beckon me to remember his mercy. The Lord grants me forgiveness when I am at fault and asks only that I try sincerely to be faithful to him. Each time I repent, I grow less centered on myself and more submissive to him. There may be faults in me that I do not yet see: selfish motivations, false guilt feelings, self-deceptions. I can try to work these through in accordance with the teachings of the Church, but if I fail I must be confident of the unchanging gift of God's mercy and forgiveness. He calls me to repent for those sins I know about and those faults I only vaguely suspect.

In moments when I feel most unsure, I must remember to ask for his guidance. I cannot profess to rely wholly on God and all the while act as if my attachment to persons and things will slake my thirst for him. Any exclusive clinging to things or persons outside of God is enough to block the true path of spiritual transformation. Anything I cling to, no matter how small, can take the place of my affection for God. Desire set on God alone strengthens my soul to see all persons and things in him; dispersed desires only weaken me in the pursuit of virtue. As long as my soul clings to what it craves immoderately, it will never make progress or reach perfection.

I especially have to be careful when these attachments are clung to under the pretext of doing good. Instead of calling attention to myself, I ought to refrain from bragging about the good I've done. I am simply to do it, whether praised or not. If I receive no thanks either directly or indirectly from those who receive my services, I must try to do the same as I have always done with joy and purity of heart. It is so human to want immediate credit for the good I do, if only a nod of thanks. Yet, following my Lord, I must free myself from any ulterior motives of self-gain and listen to the call of love, even in the face of ingratitude.

Jesus is my model for such selfless, forgiving love. He must have done many good works in secret during his hidden life. Even during his public ministry, he always fled the applause of the crowd. He performed good works solely for God's sake and to prepare people for the Kingdom.

The moment of reconciliation between God and man came when Christ was completely annihilated in everything, with respect to human reputation, to nature, to spiritual consolation. By his example, I learn that the more I am annihilated for God's sake, the more I am united to him. Only when I am reduced to nothing, as Christ was on the cross, to the extreme of humility, is there wrought between my soul and God that union of lover and Beloved which marks the culminating point of our journey in this life. Only then can I say, "Father, forgive them; they do not know what they are doing."[20]

How foolish it is, then, to think that projects of self-salvation will suffice to atone for sin. Atonement comes from Christ; I did nothing to merit this gift. Any holiness in me comes from him. All I can do is offer him my limited yet loving self, sinful yet beseeching his forgiveness.

* * *

CLOSING PRAYER

Lord, you love my poor, imperfect self.
You let me live
According to the gifts and limits you have given.
You free me from the pressure of perfecting
An impossible ideal.
In your mercy you demand of me
No more than I can bear.
By your free gift of forgiveness
You relieve the gravity of sin
If I repent sincerely.
You ask me to become
A channel of your mercy
That I may share with others
The forgiveness shown to me.
Free me from deceptive projects
That boast of self-redemption.
Purify my heart of foolish pride
And the need for constant consolation.
Grant me the grace to carry your cross
In unflinching dedication.
Place me on the path I am to follow
Freed from sin and sheltered
By your forgiving Spirit.

CHAPTER FIVE

Blessing of Affliction

We are journeying step by step into the language and living of spirituality. On this journey, we sense the interplay between such spiritual themes as simplicity, discipline, awakening, forgiveness. Words and experiences appropriate to the life of the spirit appear and reappear in Holy Scripture and the writings of spiritual masters, in personal reflection, in letters, diaries, maxims, and counsels.

Affliction seen not as a curse but as a blessing is another recurrent theme. It becomes a blessing provided I can place my pain against the horizon of faith in Christ and love for his cross. Living this paradox of affliction as a mixture of suffering and joy advances the journey to God. How can this be? How can this self-annihilating experience be of such benefit to the soul?

Some time ago I received sad news in regard to a dear friend who, up until the occasion of a serious illness, had been the picture of blooming health. She picked up a highly contagious disease on a trip she and her husband had made to the South Pacific. The cure required many months of quiet rest, in and out of hospitals. When I received word of my friend's illness,

I wrote her a letter, sections of which I include here, together with her answer, for this correspondence seems to offer a concrete example of how affliction can be a blessing from the spiritual point of view. I begin with excerpts from my letter to her:

I suspect you have found many inner resources, those more quiet streams of reflection and prayer that only have a chance to emerge when the active ego functional side has to slow down. The spiritual masters speak of suffering as a mystery of affliction. They always regard any form of sickness as a blessing in disguise—if we are able to live it with the proper attitude. I think the ancient wisdom they convey involves letting go of the ego-functional dimension, the active, sometimes willful side of me, so that the release of inner resources is possible. Literally, there is nothing to do when we are seriously ill but to be, just to be our vulnerable, dependent, non-utilitarian, gentle selves.

In the midst of suffering, at a time when we may be the lowest physically, we can allow the gentle spirit self to emerge. Remember Samuel's remark, "Here I am, Lord." Well, that's about all we can say: "Here I am, Lord." Not very efficient today, not managing everything so well, maybe misinterpreting your message . . . that's me, Lord, failing and faltering all the time, yet knowing that I try and that you see and love my trying.

It is so amazing to discover the kinds of thoughts that are released when our bodies fail us in some way. Perhaps this is why spiritual writers speak of the blessing of affliction. It is a real blessing, for at such moments we can sort out better than ever the essential from the peripheral, the important from the unimportant, the ultimate from the temporal. I think in such moments we come closer to God and I believe that if times of sickness are lived to their fullest, that is, lived in such a way that we "own" deeply and without fear our temporality, then life after that takes on a new glow. We are made softer somehow by such an experience if we live it in the proper receptive mood; otherwise it can make us hard and bitter and depressed. But, if we live it gently, then times like these can have a profound effect on our lives. Because of this experience, we can see anew; we appreciate the most tiny moments of life, the incredible beauty of nature, the utter ongoingness of everything and our small but unrepeatable role.

I had a taste of this feeling when I lay sick after two surgeries, feeling drained and weak from medication and loss of blood. Life is so good and yet we realize we have to let go and, letting go, it becomes even better. Why? Because we are less grasping, less feeling we always have to prove something, less needful of being in control. Letting go, we let ourselves into the hands of God and realize that it is all right to be held and carried and redeemed . . .

Here is my friend's answer. She writes first about what she calls that "exquisite stage of surrendering."

I had in no way fought my disease. Never was I resentful or even questioning as to why it should have come to me. I truly looked upon it as an adventure, as an artistic experience, that would open new doors, afford fresh insight.

This was her first response. It changes a little later.

I was filled with gratitude for my magnificent surroundings—the river to gaze upon, the wild life to observe. Being ill brought me into a kind of communion with all the others who are suffering physically; I felt even deeper gratitude to God that my trial was so slight, so heavily compensated, and, of course, I wrote you what joy I was finding in the long hours for reading and study. Because my days were so filled with reading, making notes, digesting and assimilating new ideas, writing long letters to a few dear friends, I hadn't a moment's depression which is a regular symptom of this disease. I never even longed to go on a picnic with the boys and their friends. There wasn't a moment's sadness in seeing them loaded down with instruments and headed for town; even missing my beloved pack trip into the Wind River wilderness was not a disappointment.

I was astonished by the richness of my memory of past trips up there in that piercing clear light, with those awesome views from the top of the peak, ridge after ridge of mountains, the sight of an emerald lake surrounded by granite cliffs, the sound of icy torrents of water pouring out of high crevices; but in spite of all of these good gifts God was working in me through my illness, there was a tremendous gulf between the letting go that I assumed I was doing and my strong controlling ego; though I kept my bones between those sheets constantly for one month, and then with only brief trips into the kitchen and being at the table for the evening meal, I still managed to involve myself with the many unnecessary details of the household, worrying about all manner of things. As my brother-in-law put it, everything went through "control center," which is what he called my four-poster bed—whether it was a sick horse, a dead steer, a battered pick-up, the broken icebox, the burnt out element in the oven, the well water changing and turning our silver orange!

Now you can see . . . how much I need the practice and daily commitment of letting go totally. I am slowly inching along in this strange and yet thrilling approach. Without having been grounded in the essence of his [Adrian van Kaam's, *Spirituality and the Gentle Life*] message, I could never even attempt it because he always so beautifully keeps the fine line of spirit, body and ego balanced. Nevertheless, his message has stopped me in my tracks, made me see the folly of my ego control, of my deep reluctance to being my "vulnerable, dependent, non-utilitarian gentle self," which is how you phrased it in your letter.

I guess one problem was that I just wasn't quite sick enough. God's wisdom has even taken care of that. I am back in the Salt Lake Hospital with what the doctors call chronic aggressive hepatitis; already one-fourth of my liver is destroyed, and had I lived a decade or so ago I would be gone in a matter of months. The doctor is confident that within six months the whole process will be stopped. It all sounds rather grim but it isn't, mostly because of the

insights . . . given me in the past . . . Starting today I
am allowed to dress and walk around the block and I
have all along been allowed to go to Mass in the
chapel just down the hall from my room.

The first onset of the disease was regarded by my
friend as an adventure, in her words, "an artistic
experience." Because of her religious background, she
felt a certain gratitude, communion, and joy rather
than the usual depression that accompanies this
disease. Added to these religious feelings was a
richness of memory that seemed to accompany her
affliction and suffering. Still she felt a gulf between
letting go totally and her ego tendency to control.
Gradually she began to see what she calls the folly of
her doing side versus being her vulnerable, dependent, gentle self. Recurrent and more serious illness
teaches her the lesson that affliction lived in peaceful
surrender to God's will can advance the flight of my
soul to him. He grants the inner strength needed to
transform suffering into joy.

We do not necessarily have to come down with a
contagious disease to experience this paradox of
affliction. Spiritual reading can itself be an occasion
for suffering because it forces us to reexamine our
priorities; it may draw forth the same kind of self-
reflection that happens when we are in a sick bed.
Something in the text may prompt us to reevaluate our
way of life. When we do serious spiritual reading, we

may begin to understand what it actually means to walk the way of the cross. It is not enough to weaken our ego temporarily due to sickness; gradually we must release all vestiges of control; all ego possessiveness must be whittled away so that we can let go totally and let ourselves into the hands of God.

The genuine friend of the cross seeks, in St. John's words, the distasteful rather than the delectable; he leans more toward suffering than sweet consolation; he prefers going without everything for God's sake than being trapped by possessions. Following this road does not entail a multiplicity of methods of mortification and prayer. To follow the way requires one thing only, almost painful in its simplicity, and that is denial of self for Christ's sake. In this "dark night" the soul experiences afflictions and benefits, both of which St. John describes.

Afflictions of the Dark Night

To bring this description of the dark night and its afflictions and blessings closer home, I want to consider side by side with St. John's analysis the life experience of a fellow sufferer, a man named Jacques Fesch, who, like my friend, learned through suffering to surrender wholly to God's will.[1] Jacques' story is told through a series of letters that he wrote while in a French prison, awaiting the outcome of his trial for the crimes of theft and murder. After about two and a half years in the Sante prison, he was led to the scaffold, executed for his crimes but extraordinarily graced by God.

During the time of his confinement, Jacques underwent in rather rapid succession the stages of spiritual transformation from purgation to union. He died a dignified and happy death, assured by Christ of his salvation. Jacques' life prior to his arrest had been by all outward signs a miserable failure. The child of a loving but weak mother, a coldly authoritative and cynical father, young Jacques soon gave in to his tendencies to laziness, misconduct, and paralyzing discouragement. He married a young girl, Pierrette, whom he had made pregnant, but soon after—despite a genuine affection for her and their daughter, Veronica, he abandoned the family and returned to his mother's home. When a business venture failed, he did not know where to turn in the real world and so escaped into the realm of fantasy, of floating plans and projects. Here he conceived of getting together enough money to buy a boat and make an around-the-world voyage. The plan obsessed him. He could think of nothing but his boat. He was a man driven by a fantasy, no longer a free, reflective being but an impulsive set of reactions. In this state, he attacked and robbed a money-changer, made his escape pursued by a policeman, and, when cornered in a courtyard, turned, shot, and killed his pursuer.

Arrested and put in prison, a wreck physically and psychologically, Jacques' spiritual trial was about to begin.

In letters to his wife, his lawyer, his mother-in-law, and a priest-friend, Jacques traces the stages of his conversion and spiritual rebirth, of his progress on the way of spiritual deepening, his trial, hour of darkness, and entrance to the light. Locked in solitary confinement most of the time, he has no one to talk to but God and the people he corresponds with. Early letters reveal no vain attempt to justify his crime. He realizes he acted like an irrational creature and, though not responsible for his actions, he does take responsibility for their evil consequences. He acknowledges before God his weakness and sin. He does not try to cover up his humiliation by excuses. Something tells him he has to choose between introspectively blaming the past (his childhood, his education, his parents) for what happened to him or letting go of this wretched history in true forgiveness and going on from there. Prompted by grace, he chooses the latter course. This choice prepares him for his conversion.

Because he has been brought so low, Jacques has to forsake his foolish attempts to arouse faith by reason and simply turn over to Christ his whole suffering self. This he does and the Lord quickly elevates him from disbelief to faith. Conversion softens Jacques' stony heart, but he realizes intuitively that his inner trial is far from over. This initial surrender, followed by a felt experience of Jesus' presence, must now be purged and tested in the crucible of faith. Jacques has found peace, but he has found war at the same time. The further he moves on the spiritual road, the more clearly he sees the depths of his wretchedness. He discovers that these temporary touches of God are not ends in themselves but means toward the permanent spiritual reform God would require.[2]

To bring him to this state of light, God would have to lead Jacques into that dark night which, in the deepest sense, refers to an inflow of God into the soul.[3] This inflow purges one of deeply ingrained bad habits, of attitudes of pride, discouragement, sloth that Jacques knew so well. God infuses this divine light in darkness to prepare the soul for a union that surpasses all self-sufficient efforts. This night of affliction and torment aims to purge and illumine. In Jacques' words:

> . . . with the testing comes faith, and with the faith the graces that are distributed not in a niggardly way but with a generous hand. The yoke becomes sweet and sorrow changes into joy; what is hidden from men's eyes becomes luminously clear to anyone whom the Lord draws. . . .[4]

Why is this dark night at once so full of blessings and so afflictive? St. John answers, and Jacques attests, that this night causes pain because it exceeds the soul's capacity to understand. ". . . those who live in the world find all this very difficult to comprehend . . . There is no coherence in it to the eye of the mere spectator."⁵ God's presence, the bright ray of his wisdom, as St. John repeats, causes "thick darkness" in the intellect. He offers the comparison that when eyes are sickly, impure, and weak, they suffer pain if a bright light shines upon them. "When this pure light strikes in order to expel all impurity, a person feels so unclean and wretched that it seems God is against him and that he is against God."⁶ Jacques' experience is amazingly similar. Though believing fully in God, he thinks he has been rejected by him. He suffers the pain and grief of Job in the worst of his trials.⁷

> To belong to a God of light and yet live in darkness, to possess in one's heart who is Love itself and yet feel oneself to be as cold as marble: that is desolation such as *no one can understand who has not experienced it.*⁸

Seen against the background of this divine and dark light, the misery and impurity of the soul seems overwhelming. A profound sense of nothingness pervades the soul. Jacques sees his moral and spiritual weakness as never before. In light of God's goodness, he feels wholly unworthy and out of his favor. He wonders, as Job did, who will take pity on him now

that God has touched him?[9] Only gradually will it
become clear that the aim of God in this touch is not
meant to chastise the soul but to grant it innumerable
favors. The habitual affections and attachments of the
old Jacques are being stripped away by divine wisdom
in order to renew his soul and divinize it. The results
of this rebirth process are not felt immediately. For
now, the soul remains in the dying phase—in
profound darkness—feeling as if it is "melting away
and being undone by a cruel spiritual death."[10]

> My life is an unending series of ups and downs.
> January and February were a time of spiritual
> euphoria that was a great help in my search for God;
> then, at the beginning of March, total darkness fell on
> me again. Initially, I found strength in the forward
> movement which the previous two months had oc-
> casioned; now I just drag myself painfully along with
> many sighs and cries for help. God certainly is in-
> tending to test me and thinks that this state of
> seeming abandonment is more profitable for my
> future salvation and progress. . . .[11]

The shadow of death, the sighs and sorrows that
encircle the soul—all reflect the feeling of God's
absence, of being chastised and rejected by him, of
being unworthy of him and the object of his anger.
Despite the support of family members and friends,
Jacques feels at times forsaken and despised—an
outcast among men. On the sensory level, feelings of

"spiritual euphoria" are forced out by pervasive aridity. In regard to the spiritual faculties, reasoning powers fail to provide answers. Memory only brings to mind more evidence of his abject misery. Will is suspended from the refreshment and delight that accompanies the felt possession of God.

The anguish of being in this darkness is comparable to "hanging in midair, unable to breathe."[12] The sinful habits contracted throughout Jacques' life are being annihilated and consumed as "fire consumes the tarnish and rust of metal."[13] Little wonder, then, that he experiences such inner torment and debates if God will ever free him from the power of death.[14] Jacques learns gradually that there is a divine purpose for all this pain. St. John keeps pointing to it. "God humbles the soul greatly in order to exalt it greatly afterwards."[15] He allows these afflictions in their intensity to occur at intervals, knowing that the soul can bear only so much. Thus Jacques' "ups and downs." The purgation endures for a longer or shorter time, with greater or lesser force, depending on the degree of union that God in his mercy desires to grant the soul. It may take some years for the soul to become humbled, softened, and purified, so delicate, simple, and refined that it can be one with the Spirit of God. At intervals, "this dark contemplation ceases to assail the soul in a purgative mode and shines upon it illuminatively and lovingly."[16] Such has been Jacques' experience: "I find a great deal of strength in

prayer and intimate conversation with God, and
sometimes I taste the sweetness of the Lord! Then I
have a deep joy and am greatly consoled."[17]

In the midst of his trial, Jacques enjoys a taste of the
bliss God is leading him towards. This occasional
experience of God's peace and loving friendship may
be so intense that one thinks his trials are over, but
hidden roots of imperfection still remain to be purged.
Just when Jacques feels consoled and least expects it,
purgation returns to engulf him in another degree
more severe and dark than the former; he doubts
again if his afflictions will ever end.

> For myself, you see, when joy departs, I feel com-
> pletely crippled; then the "old self" revives in me with
> immense power! Everything I thought I had left far
> behind me is there in front of me again, just as in-
> fluential as before and no less serious than before. I
> must use all my strength to suppress these evil desires.
> If I am locked up here, without any source of temp-
> tation, and yet this is the way I am, what would I be if
> I were outside and free? I think—I say it to my
> shame—that I would fall back into the same
> mistakes, at least momentarily. The dog returns to its
> vomit! How weak the flesh is! At such moments I
> pray, more intensely than usually perhaps, but badly
> just the same. I always have the feeling that I am
> alone and that everything is useless.[18]

To the pain that pierces Jacques' soul when he sees
his poverty is added the remembrance of past joys.

Having known the consolation of conversion, he feels by contrast the desolation of God's seeming desertion. It seems hard to believe that there are great blessings contained in such afflictions, that God will raise up what he seems so cruelly to have cast down. The person suffering this purgation knows that he loves God, that "he would give a thousand lives for Him,"[19] but he finds no relief. No one seems to understand what he is going through. Reasons cause greater sorrow and offer no remedy "until the Lord finishes purging him in the way He desires."[20]

Something else grieves the person in this state: ". . . since this dark night impedes his faculties and affections, he cannot beseech God nor raise his mind and affections to Him."[21] To pray and at the same time to doubt that God hears or pays attention to prayer adds new torment. Jacques admits, ". . . my prayer is a weak light that hardly stands out against the darkness."[22] In the end, one can do nothing but suffer this purgation patiently, giving over, as Jacques does, his punishments and afflictions to the crucified Christ, trusting that as human understanding grows darker, the divine light will shine more brightly.

Not finding satisfaction in anything, not understanding anything in particular, waiting upon God in emptiness and darkness, the soul is ready to embrace the supernatural benefits God has been granting all along. This dark night then becomes for

Jacques, as for St. John, a "glad night," a "guiding night . . . more lovely than the dawn!"[23]

Benefits of the Dark Night

Jacques' midnight hour passes slowly into the dawn of joy. The more he embraces the cross, the less alone he feels. He experiences how infinite the love of Christ is. He begins to know, as St. John did, that if this night darkens, it does so to give light:

> . . . even though this happy night darkens the spirit, it does so only to impart light concerning all things; and even though it humbles a person and reveals his miseries, it does so only to exalt him; and even though it impoverishes and empties him of all possessions and natural affection, it does so only that he may reach out divinely to the enjoyment of all earthly and heavenly things, with a general freedom of spirit in them all.[24]

The reason for this testing is to ripen faith. God takes from the soul its swaddling clothes, puts it down from his arms, and makes it walk alone. He weans the disciple from the sweet food of infants and lets him taste the food of the strong, which, for St. John, means acceptance of the cross. Jacques likewise insists, *"We can have no genuine hope of peace and salvation apart from Christ crucified."*[25] The cross teaches us to know ourselves and our misery; it strips us of the illusion of control and makes us realize the depths of our dependence on God.

Other benefits flow from the pain of self-knowledge. Previous consolation may have made us overly bold with God and likely to take his love for granted. Now, having experienced his distance, we may approach him with more respect and discretion, desiring only what he wills and not merely what makes us feel good.

God illumines Jacques' soul not only by granting him knowledge of his own misery and lowliness but also by allowing him to know his Maker's grandeur and majesty. "My being proclaims the greatness of the Lord, my spirit finds joy in God my Savior."[26] Unhindered by self-centered desires, finding his joy in God, Jacques grows confident that never does the Lord desert him; even if he seems distant, Jesus is still near. From this sense of the Lord's nearness to him stems his sense of nearness to his loved ones, even though prison walls lie between them. Jacques feels a spontaneous outpouring of love for all men. He shares Christ's compassion for the human condition. Wretchedness only serves to heighten his awareness of God's mercy. As Jacques says in one of his last letters, "I am living through wonderful days."[27] Vital and ego longings lose their strength to bind his spirit. Despite physical suffering and the loss of power, he begins to live on the eve of his execution in spiritual sobriety, peace, and tranquillity. He tries, with God's grace, to quell impatient or angry feelings towards his accusers when he appears in court for sentencing. Charity begins to correct the bitterness he was prone to feel at the beginning of his imprisonment. Acceptance of whatever God sends prevents him from giving up in discouragement. He trusts that God is communicating his love even when he feels most dry.

> I am being tested like gold in the furnace, and that in two ways: by powerful thrusts toward the light, followed by brief periods of darkness, and by more or less lengthy periods of abandonment in which all joy has vanished and only dryness is left.[28]

While he does not seek consolation as he did before, Jacques thanks God humbly when it comes. Despite the suffering he must undergo to follow Christ, he would not want to choose an easier way.

> I can assure you that I am well aware of the depth of purification one must reach before being admitted to contemplation of the Lord! Jesus is adorning my soul, taking away even the least evil thought, sharpening my sensibilities, and enlightening my conscience so that I may collaborate with Him in His constructive work. *I have been in agony for almost two months* and can see clearly how impossible it is for those who do not make an entire submission to reach paradise. Jesus does everything and I let Him do it, even though it hurts. I am waiting for everything to be made ready; then He will gather the fruits of what He has sown and

will absorb me into contemplation of His infinite love.[29]

From this choice of the "narrow way" flows Jacques' intention to persevere until the final consummation. The love of God becomes his sole motivation during these last few days. He draws strength from Christ in his weakness. Despite his sins, he knows that the Lord is drawing him toward an eternity of happiness. A scene from the life of Jesus that comes to mean more and more to him is that of love itself hanging beside the Good Thief. Jacques feels with unwavering faith that Jesus' words to this man are being addressed personally to him: "I assure you: this day you will be with me in paradise."[30]

Jacques now awaits the moment of death when he will be lifted up into the delight of God's wisdom, the peace of his kingdom, the fire of his love. The main benefit of this night that Jacques has been through is the "vehement passion of divine love" it stirs up in the soul. According to St. John, the soul experiences a serenity of spirit so delicate and delightful that its effect is ineffable. This infused contemplation acts upon both the intellect and will; sublimely, tenderly, and forcibly it grants light and enkindles love. Jacques' desire becomes that of St. Therese of the Child Jesus: to die of love.[31] In his final notes, he writes:

I wait in the night and in peace. My eyes are intent on the crucifix, my gaze on my Saviour's wounds. I repeat without wearying: "All for you!" I want to keep the image of Him before my eyes to the end, even though I shall suffer but little. I wait expectantly for love! In five hours I shall look upon Jesus!

He is drawing me sweetly to Himself and giving me a peace which is not of this world. . . . How good Jesus is, suffering so much for me on the cross and now bearing all my pain! Happy the man who puts his trust in the Lord. He will never be deceived! God is Love![32]

Jacques loves God not only because he has been generous and good to him but because God himself is love. He showed the depths of his love by suffering for our sake. Through his suffering, our souls have been released from the bondage of sin and made ready for eternal life. Jacques knows he is going to see God face to face because Jesus' sacrifice has atoned for his sin.

A man must be as pure as Christ if he is to gaze upon Him. . . . Jesus wants to take me with Him to paradise. He can do everything in us. . . . I believe that I shall go straight to heaven.[33]

On this note of total confidence, Jacques climbed the scaffold at 5:30 A.M., on the morning of October 1, 1957. At age twenty-seven, he was decapitated and, as he deeply believed, entered into Life at the Lord's bidding.

Living the Blessings of Affliction

When my friend got sick, especially because she was used to good health, she felt powerless. She was drawn to ponder as never before the mystery of affliction; she had to let go of her habitual activities around the ranch. Anticipated events like the annual pack trip to the wilderness had to be canceled. Being "stripped" of the good times granted her a chance to reappraise what is lasting and what is passing. As physical suffering robbed her of habitual health, so spiritual suffering left her without the comfort of a complacent faith. Instead of becoming bitter and depressed when her sickness became worse, she saw this setback as God's way of teaching her to lose herself in him. A new depth of faith was called for that would silence all easy answers and the last traces of ego control. Easy answers would not solve the paradox of affliction. All she could do was to live her suffering in faith and listen to its deeper meaning on the level of spirit.

I remember once visiting an infirmary where there were many old sick nuns. There was one sister the nurses were particularly eager for me to meet. We walked into her room and I will never forget the face of this sister as she lay quietly on her bed. Her skin was like tissue paper; it was almost as if I could see right through her, so transparent did she look. She had been bedridden for fifteen years. It was obvious that she bore her suffering in Christ with the utmost dignity, joy and patience. She was happy to be there, she said, as a full-time praying member of her community. She prayed all day long for her fellow sisters and for their families and friends, for people in the world who asked for prayers. She then turned and asked me, "Do you have a special intention that you want me to include in my prayers?" There was nothing I could do, nothing I had done, to deserve her prayers. In her suffering she quietly took upon herself the added burden of my intentions.

Such people who live lives of total self sacrifice have found their true selves. They are a living answer to the mystery of affliction, a living proof that God values in us the inclination to accept suffering for love of him more than all the consolations we might receive.

Journal of the Journey

Crucified inwardly and outwardly with Christ, you will live in this life with fullness and satisfaction of soul, and possess your soul in patience.

Let Christ crucified be enough for you, and with Him suffer and take your rest, and hence annihilate yourself in all inward and outward things.

He who seeks not the cross of Christ seeks not the glory of Christ.[3 4]

+

The road I walk with my Savior when I take up his cross leads to life. What does life mean here? The way of the cross seems at first glance life-denying not life-creating. Of what value is such affliction? It seems contrary to what people mean by the good life, free of suffering and not sparing in sources of pleasure. When I follow Jesus, I do not merely look for comfort or pleasure but for what lasts when these surface goods pass away.

To walk the way of the cross means to face life as it is, to see its basic insufficiency, to go beyond the superficial, to taste the bitter with the sweet. Christ knew both tastes: the bitterness of crucifixion, the sweetness of resurrection. He went to the depths of each experience. In the bitterness of betrayal, he found the sweetness of obeying the Father's will. In the sweetness of saying *yes* to his redemptive suffering, he tasted the bitterness of knowing that many would refuse the fruits of his redemption.

Ultimately, I am called to rise above both of these experiences in the harmony of worshipful presence to the Divine Persons where neither bitter nor sweet matters. All is one: the "sweet cautery" and the "delightful wound."

> O sweet cautery,
> O delightful wound!
> O gentle hand! O delicate touch
> That tastes of eternal life
> And pays every debt!
> In killing You changed death to life.[35]

God reveals himself as God in the capacity to change death to life. By enduring the trials he sends, I can begin to discover whether my love is strong enough to last through all forms of physical and spiritual suffering. I may be able to see the wound of affliction as delightful, as a tender touch of God through which I can know my true condition and taste the promise of eternal life. I must more and more come to regard instances of chastisement and correction as signs of God's purifying love, as wounds he inflicts because he wants me to be worthy of him.

Just as it is easy to love a friend when things are going well, so, too, it is easy to love God when he is my consoling Friend, sending graces and spiritual favors. But can I love him with the same intensity when he seems to have abandoned me? When my most fervent prayers go unheard? When unexpected sufferings come my way? At such times, my love is tested. If I can truly accept this dryness, welcome this suffering as his will, and thank him for the blessing of affliction, my love will prove itself enduring and become pleasing to him. He knows I am as willing to carry his cross as to rejoice in his consolation.

To thank God for my sufferings, my disappointments, my failures is to say again and again: "I love you no matter what happens to me because you are my God, you are holy, you know what is best for my life." Such surrender brings inner tranquillity and lasting peace. It allows me to go on loving God no matter how somber the surrounding night.

* * *

CLOSING PRAYER

How easily I shun the darkness, Lord,
Forgetting you are there.
I fear the silent desert
And run from the arid night.
Why do I doubt your presence
In time of desolation?
Why do I doubt the blessing
You grant amidst affliction?
Remind me when I cannot see
In suffering you are near.
Let me welcome darkness
As much as morning light.
Teach me, Lord, to thank you
Whatever cross you send.
Though following you means
Forsaking worldly consolation
Keep me faithful to your word.
In sorrow let me bless you,
In joy exclaim my praise.

CHAPTER SIX

Tasting Eternal Happiness

The peace Jesus promises and the joy it brings is a condition the world cannot give. People spend millions trying to find the "good life," as if one can make or create happiness by sheer will power. Instead of happiness, the by-product of such effort may only be more agitation. People end up with more and more goods that seem to insure it—campers, trailers, televisions, radios, cars, exotic foods, travel to far-off places—and still happiness eludes them.

Happiness seems to mean getting more material goods. It also seems to be a marketable product. Happiness is California. Happiness is a hair coloring. Happiness is a smile, or having white teeth, or smelling good—all of these things are equated with happiness. People want to be happy, and yet we witness a great deal of depression. Side effects of the "happiness market" take the form of frustration and aggravation. Two weeks after Christmas, people plead that things don't work right. The appliance was brand new under the tree and now it needs repaired. How can they make things so cheap? We see people in various stages of stress and strain. A man is irritated with his wife; he hollers at his children; he kicks the dog. He may not know what's bugging him until he stops to reflect on the way he has become a victim of the happiness market. Others are facing crises of values and some even ponder suicide.

Happiness cannot be bought and yet my culture keeps tempting me in that direction: records, TV's, camping equipment, sex clinics, encounter groups— all are offered as a means to find "it", but the common result is "product disappointment." The typewriter breaks, the tube fizzles out in the TV, the mixer doesn't mix. Whatever the case may be, I feel really disappointed. I thought this item was going to make me happy, but now I feel deceived.

One's whole life can go that way. What if I set out to attain a goal I think will fulfill me? I refuse to let anything get in the way of that goal. Love, family relations, unexpected surprises are not allowed to interfere. I have a one track mind to achieve that goal because then I'll be happy. So I work hard to get there. I go through the proper channels, attain the right degrees, climb to the top, and at the end of it I still experience dissatisfaction. Now what? Here I am with all this status and I feel as frustrated as ever. Life doesn't make any sense. I made all those sacrifices and I feel so empty. Such is usually the result when ego becomes the center of self.

Just ask someone the question, "Why are you doing this?" and, most of the time the answer is, "I think it's going to make me happier," or "I know I'm going

to feel better," or "It's going to make my wife a
happier person." Together with the "I," the "if"
clause is attached to happiness: "If I just had a little
more money, I could be so happy" or "If my health
were better, I'd be happier."

Happiness is a motivation behind many of our
dreams, desires, and good works. These activities are
not bad in themselves. There is nothing wrong as such
in gaining status, becoming a good teacher, having
more money, striving after good health. The trouble
comes in when I make happiness directly dependent
on them.

Conditions for Happiness on Earth

The ego view that I can buy happiness or make it
happen is quite different from seeing happiness as a
gift—not as a goal reachable in itself but as an experience that emerges when I am living on the level of
Spirit, listening to God's will in the events and persons
he allows into my life, and not thinking so much about
whether this goal will make me happy or not. Happiness happens; it is an indefinable quality of presence
that somehow radiates the message of goodness, joy,
and peace.

Happiness is a human need, and yet it is not
something I can buy or will; it goes beyond anything
technology can invent or creature comforts provide. I
cannot make it happen, but I can create conditions
that may facilitate its emergence. For instance,

happiness seems to be associated with simple pleasures like gardening, reading, or sewing, with giving myself to others in a charitable act, with allowing the unexpected into my life. I think of times when I've felt really happy. It is hard to define exactly what that feeling is. Perhaps it's an overall condition of well being, a feeling that flows over one unexpectedly, a moment "after the fact" of really being with another person in friendship or doing something good. I can't explain it, but all of a sudden I feel so happy. One secret to happiness thus seems to be aiming at something else besides happiness and then finding it along the way.

Another condition for happiness in the spiritual sense seems to entail my not becoming overly attached to the goods of this world. As I loosen my grip on the finite, I can wonder at the Infinite. I can celebrate the particular without being dominated by it. I can stand in awe before the created as a manifestation of the Creator.[1] This attitude of detachment fosters in me a relaxed and playful presence to life and makes me feel happy. To reach the state of wanting nothing is to tap the source of all.

> To reach satisfaction in all
> desire its possession in nothing.
> To come to possess all
> desire the possession of nothing.[2]

This state of desirelessness, paradoxical as it may
seem, sums up the soul's ascent to happiness. My
myriad desires for things are reduced to the one desire
for God.

In the figure of Simeon, we witness a man who all
his life had only one desire: to see his Savior before he
died. In the Gospel of Saint Luke, Simeon is described
as an upright and devout man,[3] surely not a victim of
the illusion that men could save themselves. So simple
and trusting was his prayer that the Holy Spirit
assured him that he would not see death until his eyes
rested on the Messiah. When he beheld the Divine
Child, his quest for happiness would be fulfilled. We
can imagine how Simeon's heart must have pounded
with joy when he heard this news. Times were not easy
for the old man and many thoughts must have filled
his head when he was prompted by the Spirit to come
to the Temple. The flavor of his reflection is captured
in T.S. Eliot's poem, "A Song for Simeon."[4]

> Lord, the Roman hyacinths are blooming in bowls
>   and
> The winter sun creeps by the snow hills;
> The stubborn season has made stand.
> My life is light, waiting for the death wind,
> Like a feather on the back of my hand.
> Dust in sunlight and memory in corners
> Wait for the wind that chills toward the dead land.
>
>   Grant us thy peace.

I have walked many years in this city,
Kept faith and fast, provided for the poor,
Have given and taken honour and ease.
There went never any rejected from my door.
Who shall remember my house, where shall live my
     children's children
When the time of sorrow is come?
They will take to the goat's path, and the fox's home
Fleeing from the foreign faces and the foreign swords.

The tone of this reflection is melancholic. Simeon feels
the "death wind" brushing against the back of his
hand. He seeks happiness in the gift of God's peace.
Though he may experience deep within its soothing
promise, on the surface he feels humanly concerned
about how pleasing he has been to God, about
whether his family is amply provided for, about what
will happen when, as he foresees, foreign soldiers will
overrun his land. Still Simeon makes his way to the
temple, thinking and praying:

Before the time of cords and scourges and la-
     mentation
Grant us thy peace.
Before the stations of the mountain of desolation,
Before the certain hour of maternal sorrow,
Now at this birth season of decease,
Let the Infant, the still unspeaking and unspoken
     Word,
Grant Israel's consolation
To one who has eighty years and no to-morrow.

Simeon prays again for peace. He foresees soon enough the time of sorrow and lamentation when the world's Savior will climb the "mountain of desolation." Now he prays to see the Infant whose presence alone can give him some taste of eternal happiness and offer consolation to the promised land. Still meditating, the old man crosses the threshold of the Temple, not knowing if today will be the day or not, but compelled by the Spirit to go there. He enters and the parents of Jesus rise and place the child in his arms. A sensation of peace and joy passes through him. He knows this is the child he has been waiting for, this is the "still unspeaking and unspoken Word."

"Now, Master, you can let your servant go in peace,
just as you promised;
because my eyes have seen the salvation
which you have prepared for all the nations to see,
a light to enlighten the pagans
and the glory of your people Israel."[5]

In Jesus' light the old man is filled with light. He blesses the holy family and utters a prophecy Jesus' mother will never forget. Here is Eliot's version of the Scripture text:

According to thy word.
They shall praise Thee and suffer in every generation
With glory and derision,

Light upon light, mounting the saints' stair,
Not for me the martyrdom, the ecstasy of thought and
    prayer,
Not for me the ultimate vision.
Grant me thy peace.
(And a sword shall pierce thy heart,
Thine also.)
I am tired with my own life and the lives of those after
    me,
I am dying my own death and the deaths of those after
    me.
Let thy servant depart,
Having seen thy salvation.

In the midst of his joy, Simeon suddenly grows sad. He sees beyond this serene moment to the lives and deaths of those who shall be influenced by this Divine Child. Some will climb to the heights of ecstasy on the mountaintop of transfiguration. Others will ponder wondrous thoughts never before known by man. Simeon can now depart from this earth into everlasting bliss, but Jesus' work has just begun. He will be the prince of glory and the victim of derision. A few will praise him, but many more will persecute him and his followers. Simeon sees that he is destined for the rising and the fall of many - -a light for those with eyes to see, a sign to be rejected by those who lack transcendent vision. Sad, too, shall be Mary's heart as she watches people kill her son. The sword that will pierce her heart will pierce others, too. All this Simeon sees, but because he has also seen the ultimate

goodness of God, he can never despair. Though he
may in the twilight of his life not mount the saints'
stair, others shall. There shall be a multitude of
servants like himself who depart peacefully, having
seen their salvation. Jacques Fesch's last words echo
the words of all who die and rise with Jesus:

Blessed Virgin, be at my side!

I am happy. . . . Farewell until we meet before God![6]

Steps to Eternal Happiness

In *The Dark Night,* St. John describes the stages of
the "saints' stair" and discloses "how secret is the way
and ascent to God and how it differs from human
knowledge."[7] He shows how this infused loving
knowledge both illumines and enamours the soul,
elevating it step by step unto God and eternal happiness with him.

The first step on the ladder of divine love finds the
soul languishing for God and losing its desire for
things that are good, but not God. It becomes in-
creasingly impossible for the enamoured soul to find
satisfaction, support, consolation, or rest in anything
in isolation from the Divine. This restlessness leads
the soul to the second step where one searches for God
unceasingly. Just as a bride looks for her beloved at all
times, so the soul turns immediately to God. Eating,
sleeping, keeping vigil, or doing anything else—all her

care is centered on the One she seeks. The soul's ascent to the third step is marked by the performance of good works through which she radiates the fervor of love she feels for her Beloved. Because his love for God was growing more intense, Jacques, too, felt deeply pained about the little he could do for the Lord in prison. He thought of himself as far worse than others who seemed to be doing more of what God deserves than he could. This attitude removes from the soul vainglory, presumption, and condemnation of others and grants one the courage to ascend to the next stage.

Here, on the fourth step, one experiences an habitual yet unwearisome suffering on account of the Beloved. Love makes all that seemed heavy light; the spirit possesses enough energy on this step to bring flesh, corrupted by sin, under control. In no way does one seek consolation from God as a condition for loving him. Jacques, especially as the end drew near, was content with what God sent. He did not besiege his Savior with requests for anything other than what he willed. All his care was directed toward how he might give some pleasure to God and render him some service because of the favors he has bestowed. God may reward such love by granting the soul moments of spiritual delight; so immense is the love of Christ that he cannot long endure the sufferings of his servant without some response to them. This fourth step so enflames and enkindles the person with desire for God that he ascends to the fifth step.

On this rung of the ladder, love imparts an impatient desire and longing for God. So ardent is the desire to apprehend the Beloved and be united to him that any delay, no matter how slight, seems long, annoying, and tiresome. In Simeon's words, "I am tired with my own life and the lives of those after me. . . . Let thy servant depart, /Having seen thy salvation." The soul seemingly faints with longing and must either see its love or die. The sixth step makes the soul run swiftly toward God by reason of its hope. Each touch invigorates it further to fly swiftly to its heart's desire. Due to the swiftness of love on this step, the soul's charity increases. Love of God flows out into love of neighbor and soon brings one to the next step.

Now that the soul's love is purified, it experiences toward God an "ardent boldness." At this stage love is so inflamed that it "neither profits by the judgment to wait nor makes use of the counsel to retreat, neither can it be curbed through shame."[8] The soul grows daring because it perceives "the divine favor of the king's scepter held out toward it."[9] From the free hand of God comes the eighth step on which the soul captures the Beloved and is united with him. This union is granted for only short periods of time since the soul has not yet climbed to the step of the perfect.

On the ninth step, the soul burns gently and interiorly with love of God. "The Holy Spirit produces this gentle and delightful ardor by reason of the perfect soul's union with God."[10] St. John says it is impossible to speak about the goods and riches of God that one enjoys on this step. Even Jacques finds it difficult to put these touches of union into words. All he can say is that he waits expectantly for love: ". . . I wait to become intoxicated by torrents of delight and to sing eternal praises to the glory of the risen Lord. . . . God is Love!"[11] The saints could write many books about such moments, but the truth behind them would still be left unsaid.

This stage of love is succeeded by the tenth and final step which is no longer in this life: ". . . love assimilates the soul to God completely because of the clear vision of God which a person possesses as soon as he reaches it."[12] Jacques was fully convinced that he would see God face to face. Since the souls of the just have been already purged through love in this life, St. John says they do not enter purgatory. They enjoy immediately the Beatific Vision, which is the cause of the soul's likeness to God. On this last step of clear vision, where God rests, nothing is any longer hidden from the soul because of its total assimilation according to its capacity to the divine essence. The soul has at last completed its journey to the happiness and home that is God's greatest gift to man.

JOURNAL OF THE JOURNEY

. . . be content only with His companionship, that you might discover in it every happiness. Even though the soul may be in heaven, it will not be happy if it does not will this deliberately. And we will be unhappy with

God, even though He is always with us, if our heart is not alone, but attached to something else.[13]

For he who is poor in spirit is happier and more constant in the midst of want, because he has placed his all in nothingness, and in all things he thus finds freedom of heart. O happy nothingness, and happy hiding place of the heart! For the heart has such power that it subjects all things to itself; this it does by desiring to be subject to nothing and losing all care so as to burn the more in love.[14]

+

To be happy is to live every moment in openness to God's loving will, to the minute by minute manifestations of his care. The "secret formula" for this kind of willing is absolute detachment from all that is not God; it involves emptying myself of every desire except that of knowing him and obeying his will.

Jesus shows me the way into this desert of interior detachment; he teaches me how to be in the world without losing sight of the Father's will, how to take pleasure in the glories of creation and yet keep sight of the Creator as their origin.

In the "happy hiding place of the heart," temporal life points to life eternal.[15] Everything falls in place. I understand more clearly what he asks and why I cannot refuse his request. I know that he is incapable of willing anything but my good. I experience the depth of his mercy, clemency, compassion.

Strong, sublime, and delicate—such is his love, constant and pure. How can I refuse this God anything? How could I not offer him my whole life to do with as he wills? He who has given me eyes to see the harmonious consonance of his world. Ears to hear the strain of symphonic sound filling the night air. Fingers to fondle the soft face of a child. How wonderfully God has made me to see, hear, feel, and taste the goodness of his creation.

He gives me not only the light of reason but also that of faith. With this light I can find him, even in darkness. In the mirror of God's unchanging love, I can see my lack of faith, my pride, my useless worry, my feeble efforts to save myself. It is this weak and sinful person who comes before the Lord. He is the daystar at the end of every night, the beginning and end of my journey. Even before I turn again to him, he comes forth to meet me in tenderness and care.

Jesus' word, through the mediation of the spiritual master, has begun to awaken me to the true meaning of happiness. What matters after all is dying to myself and allowing him to live in me. When my body makes its demands, when my impatience gets the best of me, when my lack of kindness reasserts itself, instead of becoming discouraged, I must trust in his word and its power to transform my life. If I can overcome my stubborn refusal to listen, his word will guide me home. God wants to help me on this journey. He will meet me more than halfway if I take a few steps toward him. Happily I can immerse myself in the deep things of God and celebrate each day as a revelation of his love.

* * *

CLOSING PRAYER

Lord, your love sustains me
At each turn of the road.
Gently and lovingly,
You awaken my soul.
You await my turning
And forgive my weakness,
You never forget
The likeness between us.

The most common acts
Of breathing and eating,
Speaking and praying,
Caring and teaching,
Become invitations for inner awakening,
For seeing, though darkly,
Your outpouring of graces.

Total surrender to your holy will,
Frees me from worry
And lets me grow still.
In these many faces,
I see that Most Dear,
In these many voices,
Only yours do I hear.

Make me mindful of what Christ would do,
How he would respond on each occasion.
What care and compassion would he manifest?
How can he become the source of my yes?
Yes to the Father,
Yes to the Son,
Yes to the Spirit,
To all Three in One.

This yes is the imprint you've made on my soul
The flame of love that burns deeply within,
The yes that makes possible the no to sin.
No to the old man
Gives way to the new,
Empty of self and ready for you.

Lord, unclutter my heart of worldly desires,
Enkindle within the holy fires
That light the way from here to there,
That seal this bond of likeness most rare,
That lead me to the home you've made
The life that begins beyond the grave.

EPILOGUE

Journey's End

Having come to the end of our journey, we may now be able to profit from St. John's insights regarding what may draw advanced souls off the road.[1] He says there are three "blind men" who can cause us to detour from the path God has ordained us to follow if we are to reach the perfection of his law and our faith. These are: the spiritual director, the devil, and the soul itself.

The Spiritual Director. If I desire to advance in recollection, I must take care into whose hands I entrust myself because "the disciple will become like the master."[2] Besides being learned and discreet, the director should be experienced. Knowledge and discretion are necessary but perhaps even more important is his personal experience of "what true and pure spirit is."[3] Especially where the sublime parts of this journey are concerned, I may not find a guide who can meet all my needs. If the director should unfortunately not understand the ways and properties of the spirit, he may direct me back to stages that are serviceable only to beginners, to stages he has read about or used himself.

Even though God desires to lead me to higher reaches of the life of prayer, the director may block my way by keeping me at the stage of making acts and discursive reflections sustained by the activity of the imagination. God may be drawing my soul toward the state of contemplation; he is becoming the agent of this action and I the receiver. I may be diverted from the peaceful and quiet good secretly being given to my spirit. An unschooled and inexperienced director can mar God's work at this point. To prevent this from happening, St. John advises the director how to be most helpful.

> When a person approaches this state, strive that he become detached from all satisfaction, relish, pleasure, and spiritual meditations, and do not disquiet him with cares or solicitude concerning heavenly things, and still less earthly things. Bring him to as complete a withdrawal and solitude as possible, for the more solitude he obtains and the nearer he approaches this idle tranquillity, the more abundantly will the spirit of divine wisdom be infused into his soul. This wisdom is loving, tranquil, solitary, peaceful, mild, and an inebriator of the spirit, by which the soul feels tenderly and gently wounded and carried away, without knowing by whom, nor from where, nor how. The reason is that this wisdom is communicated without the soul's own activity.[4]

Neither director nor directee may understand the refined and delicate quality of these "anointings and shadings of the Holy Spirit." That is why it is a serious and regrettable situation when in the name of spiritual

direction one damages the workmanship of the Holy
Spirit by a coarse hand; such a director "like a
blacksmith, knows no more than how to hammer and
pound with the faculties;"[5] he knows no more than
how to meditate. Not understanding the stages of
prayer nor the ways of the spirit, he gives completely
wrong advice, saying, "Come, now, lay aside these
rest periods, which amount to idleness and a waste of
time; take and meditate and make interior acts, for it
is necessary that you do your part; this other method is
the way of illusions and typical of fools."[6] He tries to
force the soul who has already attained to spirit to
walk the path of the senses. All his advice succeeds in
doing is making the soul grow more distracted, for
". . . by the activity of his natural operations, a
person loses inner solitude and recollection and,
consequently, the sublime image God was painting
within him."[7]

Because of the harm he can do to God's work, the
director should reflect that he is not the chief agent,
guide, and mover of souls in this matter. The Holy
Spirit is. The director is an instrument for guiding the
Holy Spirit's work to perfection through faith and the
law of God according to the unique spirit God gives
each directee. The director should not accommodate
souls to his method and condition but should observe
the road along which God is leading them. If he does
not recognize the way, he should humbly step aside

and let one more knowledgeable and experienced than he lead.

The director should conduct the directee as God calls him into greater solitude, tranquillity, and freedom of spirit. He should give the soul a lot of latitude so that when God introduces him into this solitude, he does not bind his corporal or spiritual faculties to some particular inner or outer object. The director should assure the person that even if he seems to be doing nothing, God is doing something to him. God, like the sun, stands above uncluttered souls ready to shine upon them and communicate himself. He will construct supernaturally in each soul the edifice he desires, if the director prepares the ground by helping the directee to strive to renounce, according to the will, all corporal and temporal things; to go forth in that faith that is darkness to the intellect; and to void the memory of forms and figures that can never grasp the formless and figureless God.

Directors who do not know what spirit is, therefore, do great injury to God; they show him disrespect by intruding with a rough hand where he is working. Directors who do not want the soul to rest and remain quiet but always want it to work, do not allow room for God's work, which is to feed the spirit "without the activity of the senses because neither the sense nor its function is capable of spirit."[8]

St. John is willing to concede that these directors err

with good will; they may be zealous and not know any better; still they should not be excused for counsels given rashly, without first understanding the road and spirit God may be asking the directee to follow. They are guilty for rudely meddling in something they do not understand instead of leaving the matter in the hands of one who does.

Not everyone knows all the happenings and stages of the spiritual journey, nor is everyone spiritually so perfect as to know every state of the interior life in which a person must be conducted and guided. At least the director should not think that he has all the requirements, or that God will not want to lead the soul further on.[9]

The director as "hewer" guides the soul to contempt of the world and mortification of its appetites; as "carver" he introduces it to holy meditations, but it takes more than hewing and carving to lead it to the ultimate perfection of the spiritual journey. God leads each soul along different paths, and not to allow for these differences leads to some of the worse methods used by "blind" directors.

For instance, God may be anointing the directee with holy desires and motives for renouncing the world, changing his way of life and serving him alone. The director by human rationalization or on basis of his own interests or out of fear of the unknown may cause the directee to delay his course of action or even worse, tell him to put these kinds of thoughts out of his mind. As a result of such bad counsel, the director becomes an obstacle to the guidance of the Holy Spirit and will have to answer before God for the harm he has caused.

The Devil. The devil is also capable of thwarting the soul in its recollection before God. Being blind himself, he wants the soul to be blind, too. One tactic he uses when he sees the soul flying along on the wings of grace is to intrude into this withdrawal from the world clouds of knowledge and sensible satisfaction. He distracts the soul and draws it out of the solitude in which the Spirit of God is working secretly. The devil can allure the soul with a little bait (for example, instilling the thought that I should be *doing* something). Giving in to his tactics by feeding the sensory part of the self can occasion the loss of abundant spiritual riches. The devil will resort to the most devilish means ("horrors, fears, or bodily pains, or exterior sounds and noises") to draw the soul out of its sublime recollection. The advice St. John gives to the directee at this point echoes the advice he gave to the director:

> Oh, then, souls, when God is according you such sovereign favors as to lead you by the state of solitude and recollection, withdrawing you from the labors of the senses, do not revert to the senses. Abandon your activity, for if this helped you, when you were beginners, to deny the world and yourselves, now that

God favors you by being Himself the agent, it is a serious obstacle. God will feed you with heavenly refreshment since you do not apply your faculties to anything, nor encumber them, but detach them from everything, which is all you yourself have to do (besides the simple loving attentiveness in the way I mentioned above, that is, when you feel no aversion toward it). You should not use any force, except to detach the soul and liberate it, so as not to alter its peace and tranquillity.[10]

The Soul Itself. The person on the spiritual path becomes his own worse enemy when, by not understanding the ways God uses to advance his journey, he disturbs and does harm to himself. He thinks that he must act by means of the senses and discursive reflection, otherwise he is "doing nothing." When God introduces him into that emptiness and solitude where he is unable to use his faculties and make acts, he strains to do so anyway. Therefore, instead of enjoying the spiritual idleness, peace, and silence with which God is adorning him, the soul goes contrary to his direction and becomes distracted, "filled with dryness and displeasure."

It will happen that while God persists in keeping the soul in that silent quietude, it persists in its desire to act through its own efforts with the intellect and the imagination. It resembles a child who kicks and cries in order to walk when his mother wants to carry him, and thus neither allows his mother to make any headway nor makes any himself; or it resembles one who moves a painting back and forth while the artist is at work so that either nothing is accomplished or the painting is damaged.[11]

To cooperate with God would entail realizing that even if I do not seem to be making progress in this quietude or doing anything, I am advancing much faster than if I were treading along on foot, for God is carrying me. Now is the time to walk at God's pace, even if I don't feel as if I am walking at all. Now is the time to abandon myself into God's hands and not my own—nor those of those other two "blind men." To abandon myself to him in this solitude and suspension of faculties is, in St. John's words, to "advance securely."

> When the soul frees itself of all things and attains to emptiness and dispossession concerning them, which is equivalent to what it can do of itself, it is impossible that God fail to do His part by communicating Himself to it, at least silently and secretly. It is more impossible than it would be for the sun not to shine on clear and uncluttered ground. As the sun rises in the morning and shines upon your house so that its light may enter if you open the shutters, so God, who in watching over Israel does not doze (Ps. 120:4), nor still less sleep, will enter the soul that is empty, and fill it with divine goods.[12]

How strange that the One for whom I have been searching has been with me all along. At no moment does he leave me; to find him all I have to do is turn within and call his name. Guided by St. John, I can begin to sense what in dark moments I may have doubted, that he is near, nearer than anything I can touch or see. He is everywhere and in everything. Nothing that is, is apart from him. Every person, place and thing calls me home to the house of my Father, if I will only stop long enough to listen. I realize again in this light the depth of surrender that is asked of me. All thoughts of self in isolation from him must be effaced so that in my heart God alone can reign.

> O lamps of fire!
> In whose splendors
> The deep caverns of feeling,
> Once obscure and blind,
> Now give forth, so rarely, so exquisitely,
> Both warmth and light to their Beloved. [13]

God is to my soul a lamp of omnipotence, of wisdom, of goodness, leading me by slow steps and, at times, great leaps back to himself. My soul can no more resist the attractiveness of his living flame than an insect on a summer's night can resist the glow of light on the porch. My soul is drawn irresistably to its own center, who is God.

The more deeply I am imbued with his love, the more I can see clearly that every blessing, early and late, great and small, comes from my Lord. The purpose of all these gifts is to bring me back to the center of myself where I dwell already in nearness to him. This centering is a prelude to that final passing when the soul leaves the life of flesh and enters the perfect life of spirit in Christ.

St. John calls these splendors, graces, and favors that God grants to the soul "overshadowings."[14] To think of God overshadowing me calls to mind images of solicitous care, awakened concern, protective vigilance. I know God in this image as a person who befriends and protects me, as the power of the Most High overshadowed Mary.

Because I live always in the shadow of God, I can to a degree experience his divine wisdom and glory. These attributes of God are lamps that cast shadows on me and make me more at one with him, who is the Goodness of my goodness, the Delight of my delight.

Far beyond all telling is this union with the Divine, when the lamps of fire become one with the Living Flame, when the shadows of many selves are reabsorbed in their Source and all becomes Light. Words fail; they break against the shores of infinity. The soul can only surrender to the waves of eternal truth and be carried where they lead. It is good to forget ego ambitions and vital desires, to lie back and float upon the waves of these words, letting them carry me, by whatever route, to the Divine Word. These words have the power to lead me home, depending on how I listen.

Words fail to describe what it is like when the soul is transformed in God, when I walk intimately with him in a bond of sweet and loving friendship. This friendship, this intimacy with the Divine, brings me to the end of my journey homeward. It grants me simplicity of presence to God in faith.

The journey homeward leads me to the birthplace of a tiny babe in Bethlehem. It leads me to Calvary. It leads me to an open tomb. In Bethlehem I witness God emptying himself and entering human history to teach me what I must do to find and live the Father's will. I realize anew that whatever takes me away from that humble stable in Bethlehem takes me away from God. On Calvary I learn that unity with the Father is not attained by displays of human power but by poverty of spirit. At the open tomb I am taken up in Christ and given the grace of life eternal. He invites me to grow strong in his love so that I may enjoy forever the blissful unity of my heavenly home. It is this love that makes possible my stepping on the path; it is this love that leads me to my journey's end.

* * *

FOOTNOTES

FOREWORD

1. Susan Annette Muto, *Approaching the Sacred: An Introduction to Spiritual Reading* (Denville, N.J.: Dimension Books, 1973).

2. Susan Annette Muto, *Steps Along the Way: The Path of Spiritual Reading* (Denville, N.J.: Dimension Books, 1975); see also, by the same author, *A Practical Guide to Spiritual Reading* (Denville, N.J.: Dimension Books, 1976).

3. Clearly, of course, one must be cautious when reading the subtle spiritual and psychological analysis of the mystical way offered by St. John. Hopefully, the interpretation of his writing presented here and elsewhere will help to offset the tendency to suppress the vital and ego dimensions of the self in the name of spiritual deepening. St. John presupposes that his "beginner" is already living an integrated spiritual life and has been elevated by God to the threshold of infused contemplation. Hence to read his writings presupposes a certain advancement in the spiritual life and, if possible, an introduction by a director into the depth of his message in order to avoid the danger of illusion. Important cautions about and prefaces to a spiritual reading of St. John can be found in the following sources: Francis Libermann, *Spiritual Letters to Clergy and Religious,* Volume Two (Pittsburgh, Pa.: Duquesne University Press, 1964), pp. 235-244; Thomas Merton, "Light in Darkness. The Ascetic Doctrine of St. John of the Cross," in *Disputed Questions* (New York: The New American Library, A Mentor-Omega Book, 1965), pp. 160-167 and, by the

same author, *The Ascent to Truth* (New York: The Viking Press, Compass Books, 1959), wherein the author presents a fuller exposition of the doctrine of St. John; and Karl Rahner, "Reflections on the Problem of the Gradual Ascent to Christian Perfection," in *Theological Investigations,* Volume III, "The Theology of the Spiritual Life," trans. Karl H. and Boniface Kruger (New York: The Seabury Press, 1974), pp. 3-23.

See also *Approaching the Sacred,* Footnote 7, p. 155.

PART ONE

PROLOGUE

1. Lk. 15:11-32. Scriptural quotes throughout this book are taken from *The Jerusalem Bible,* Reader's Edition (Garden City, N.Y.: Doubleday & Co., 1971).

2. Sacrifice gives you no pleasure,
    were I to offer holocaust, you would not have it.
    My sacrifice is this broken spirit,
    You will not scorn this crushed and broken heart.

    Ps. 51:16-17

CHAPTER ONE

SEEING SIMPLY

1. This distinction between the first and second clearness is pointed to by Baron Friedrich von Hugel in *Letters from Baron Friedrich von Hugel to a Niece,* ed. Gwendolen Greene (London: J.M. Dent & Sons, 1928), pp. 74-75.

2. See Karlfried Graf von Durckheim, *Daily Life as Spiritual Exercise: The Way of Transformation,* trans. Ruth Lewinneck and P.L. Travers (New York: Harper & Row, Publishers, Perennial Library, 1972), pp. 37-45 and, by the same author, *Hara, The Vital Centre of Man,* trans. Sylvia-Monica von Kospoth (New York; Fernhill House, 1962), pp. 140-143 and pp. 175-176 and *The Japanese Cult of Tranquility,* trans. Eda O'Shiel (London: Rider & Company, 1960), wherein the author discusses the zen exercise of "just sitting." See also Frederick Franck, *The Zen of Seeing: Seeing/Drawing as Meditation* (New York: Vintage Books, 1973).

3. St. John of the Cross, *Commentary,* Stanza 5, Paragraph 1, in *The Spiritual Canticle: The Collected Works of St. John of the Cross,* trans. Kieran Kavanaugh and Otilio Rodriguez (Washington, D.C.: Institute of Carmelite Studies, 1973), p. 434. All further references to the writings of St. John are taken from this edition and abbreviated as follows:
The Ascent of Mount Carmel—AMC
The Dark Night—DN
The Spiritual Canticle—SC
The Living Flame of Love—LFL
Sayings of Light and Love—SLL
Maxims on Love—ML
Letters—L

Books, chapters, paragraph and page numbers will be indicated accordingly.

4. SLL, 46, p. 671.

5. ML, 58, p. 678.

CHAPTER TWO

HEARING ATTENTIVELY

1. SC, Prologue, Paragraph 2, p. 409.

2. SC, *Commentary*, Stanza 1, Paragraph 3, p. 417.

3. An explanation of Russian kenoticism is offered by
    G.P. Fedotov, *The Russian Religious Mind*, Volume I,
    ed. John Meyendorff (Cambridge, Mass.: Harvard
    University Press, 1966), Chapter IV, pp. 94-131.

4. Ph. 2:5-8.

5. AMC, Book I, Chapter 13, Paragraph 6, pp. 102-103.

6. See Lk. 18:9-14.

7.   For an analysis of St. John's *Counsels To A Religious
    On How To Reach Perfection*, see *A Practical Guide to
    Spiritual Reading*, pp. 42-55.

8. SLL, 14, p. 667.

9. SLL, 31, p. 669.

10. SLL, 37, p. 670.

11. SLL, 53, p. 671.

12. See Hannah Hurnard, *The Hearing Heart* (London:
    The Olive Press, 1952).

13. LFL, Stanza 3, p. 610.

14. See Hannah Hurnard, *Hinds' Feet on High Places* (Old Tappan, N.J.: Fleming H. Revell Co., 1973) for an allegorical account of how perfect love casts out fear and frees the soul for blissful surrender to God.

CHAPTER THREE

DWELLING REPEATEDLY

1. This saying of Master Okada is related by Karlfried Graf von Dürckheim in *Hara, The Vital Centre of Man,* p. 177.

2. For further insight into the meaning and necessity of spiritual repetition, see *Steps Along the Way,* pp. 157-163, and Adrian van Kaam, *In Search of Spiritual Identity* (Denville, N.J.: Dimension Books, 1975), pp. 227-228.

3. Heb. 4:12-13.

4. SC, Stanza 35, p. 543. My italics.

5. SC, *Commentary,* Stanza 35, Paragraph 27, p. 543. My italics.

6 SC, *Commentary*, Stanza 36, Paragraph 10, p. 548.

7. SLL, 36, p. 670.

8. For an extensive description of living the desert experience, see *A Practical Guide to Spiritual Reading,* pp. 58-95.

9. See Alexander Solzhenitsyn, *The First Circle* (New York: Bantam Books, 1969) and, by the same author,

One Day in the Life of Ivan Denisovich (New York: Bantam Books, 1963).

10. For related "prison literature," the following sources are recommended: Anne Frank, *The Diary of a Young Girl,* trans. B.M. Mooyaart-Doubleday (New York: The Modern Library, 1952); Alfred Delp, *The Prison Meditations of Father Alfred Delp* (New York: The Macmillan Co., 1963); Walter J. Ciszek, with Daniel L. Flaherty, *He Leadeth Me* (Garden City, N.Y.: Doubleday & Co., 1973); Corrie Ten Boom, *The Hiding Place* (London: Hodder and Stoughton, 1971) and, by the same author, *Tramp for the Lord* (New York: Pillar Books, 1976); and *Light Upon the Scafford: The Prison Letters of Jacques Fesch,* ed., Augustin-Michel Lemonnier (St. Meinrad, Ind.: Abbey Press, 1975).

CHAPTER FOUR

WAITING PATIENTLY

1. Simone Weil, *Waiting for God,* trans. Emma Craufurd (New York: Harper & Row, Publishers, Harper Colophon Books, 1973).

2. See also *Steps Along the Way,* pp. 40-41.

3. Jb. 38:3-7 and 16-27.

4. Jb. 42:1-6.

5. Lk. 11:37-44.

6. Lk. 11:49-51.

7. Lk. 12:16-21.

8. Lk. 12:27-32.

9. ML, 1 to 5, p. 676.

10. Compare *Approaching the Sacred,* pp. 103-105.

PART TWO

CHAPTER ONE

MEETING WITH DIVINE DARKNESS

1. SC, *Commentary*, Stanza 1, Paragraph 4, p. 417.

2. Jb. 37:23-24.

3. Anonymous, *The Cloud of Unknowing* and *The Book of Privy Counseling,* ed. William Johnston (Garden City, N.Y.: Doubleday & Co., Image Books, 1973). Hereafter abbreviated CU. See "The Way of Unknowing," in *Steps Along the Way,* pp. 73-90.

4. See Is. 9:5-6.

5. AMC, Book II, Chapter 4, Paragraph 4, p. 113.

6. AMC, Book I, Chapter 13, Paragraph 4, p. 102.

7. AMC, Book II, Chapter 7, Paragraph 5, p. 123.

8. AMC, Book II, Chapter 7, Paragraph 11, p. 125.

9. Thomas à Kempis, *The Imitation of Christ,* trans. Ronald Knox and Michael Oakley (New York: Sheed and Ward, 1960), Book 4, Chapter 8, p. 196.

10. AMC, Book II, Chapter 6, Paragraph 1, p. 119.

11. AMC, Book II, Chapter 8, Paragraph 5, p. 127.

12. AMC, Book II, Chapter 9, Paragraph 1, p. 129.

13. AMC, Book II, Chapter 8, Paragraph 5, p. 128.

14. AMC, Book II, Chapter 9, Paragraph 3, p. 130.

15. AMC, Book II, Chapter 1, Paragraph 1, p. 107.

CHAPTER TWO

AWAKENING FROM ILLUSION

1. AMC, Book II, Chapter 15, Paragraph 5, p. 149.

2. For a further development of this author's spiritual self theory, see Adrian van Kaam, *The Dynamics of Spiritual Self Direction* (Denville, N.J.: Dimension Books, 1976).

3. AMC, Book I, Chapter 13, Paragraph 4, p. 102.

4. To understand the distinction between introspection and meditative reflection, see Adrian van Kaam, *In Search of Spiritual Identity,* Chapter VII, pp. 172-196.

5. AMC, Book I, Chapter 5, Paragraph 8, p. 84.

6. AMC, Book I, Chapter 6, Paragraph 3, p. 85.

7. He describes these bad effects in detail in AMC, Chapters 6 to 10, pp. 84-95.

8. AMC, Book I, Chapter 6, Paragraph 6, p. 86.

9. AMC, Book I, Chapter 6, Paragraph 6, p. 87.

10. AMC, Book I, Chapter 8, Paragraph 4, p. 90. See also Paragraph 3, p. 90 and Mt. 15:14.

11. AMC, Book I, Chapter 11, Paragraph 4, p. 97.

12. Do not suppose, my friends and sisters, that I am going to charge you to do a great many things; may it please the Lord that we do the things which our holy Fathers ordained and practised and by doing which they merited that name. It would be wrong of us to look for any other way or to learn from anyone else. There are only three things which I will explain at some length and which are taken from our Constitution itself. It is essential that we should understand how very important they are to us in helping us to preserve that peace, both inward and outward, which the Lord so earnestly recommended to us. One of these is love for each other; the second, detachment from all created things; the third, true humility, which, although I put it last, is the most important of the three and embraces all the rest.

    St. Teresa of Avila, *The Way of Perfection,* trans. E. Allison Peers (Garden City, N.Y.: Doubleday & Co., Image Books, 1964), p. 53. Hereafter abbreviated WP.

13. Let us rejoice in the communication of the sweetness of love, not only in that sweetness we already possess in our habitual union, but in that which overflows into the effective and actual practice of love, either interiorly with the will in the affective act, or exteriorly in works directed to the service of the Beloved.

    SC, *Commentary,* Stanza 36, Paragraph 4, p. 547.

14. WP, p. 73.

15. WP, p. 74.

16. WP, p. 84.

17. Lk. 18:29-30.

18. WP, p. 88.

19. See WP, p. 89. See also St. Bernard of Clairvaux, "The Steps of Humility and Pride," in *Treatises II,* trans. M. Ambrose Conway and Robert Walton (Washington, D.C.: Cistercian Publications Consortium Press, 1974).

20. See WP, Chapter 15, pp. 111-115.

21. CU, p. 65.

22. LFL, *Commentary,* Stanza 1, Paragraph 12, p. 583.

CHAPTER THREE

SPIRIT OF PRAYER

1. ML, 79, p. 680.

2. See Keith J. Egan, "Guigo II: The Theology of the Contemplative Life," in *The Spirituality of Western Christendom,* ed. E. Rozanne Elder (Kalamazoo, Mich.: Cistercian Publications, 1976), pp. 106-115.

3. St. John explains this movement in AMC, Book II, Chapters 12 to 15, pp. 136-149.

4. See St. Teresa of Avila, *The Book of Her Life,* in *The*

Collected Works of St. Teresa of Avila, Volume One, trans. Kieran Kavanaugh and Otilio Rodriguez (Washington, D.C.: Institute of Carmelite Studies, ICS Publications, 1976), Chapters 11 to 22, pp. 78-125.

5. AMC, Book II, Chapter 12, Paragraph 6, p. 138.

6. See WP, Chapters 27-42, pp. 179-280.

7. AMC, Book II, Chapter 13, Paragraph 4, p. 141.

8. AMC, Book II, Chapter 13, Paragraph 6, p. 141.

9. AMC, Book II, Chapter 13, Paragraph 7, p. 141.

10. See DN, Book I, Chapters 8 to 11, pp. 311-320.

11. DN, Book I, Chapter 8, Paragraph 3, p. 312.

12. SC, Stanza 1, p. 416.

13. SC, *Commentary,* Stanza 1, Paragraph 14, p. 422.

14. DN, Book I, Chapter 9, Paragraph 4, p. 314.

15. See DN, Book I, Chapter 9, Paragraph 5, p. 314.

16. DN, Book I, Chapter 9, Paragraph 7, p. 315.

17. DN, Book I, Chapter 9, Paragraph 8, p. 315.

18. DN, Book I, Chapter 9, Paragraph 9, p. 316.

19. See Rm. 8:26.

20. Mt. 26:41.

21. 1 Th. 5:17-18.

22. AMC, Book II, Chapter 15, Paragraph 5, p. 149.

23. See Mt. 26:36-46.

24. SLL, "Prayer of a Soul Taken with Love," p. 669.

CHAPTER FOUR

SIN AND FORGIVENESS

1. See DN, Book I, Chapters 2 to 7, pp. 299-310.

2. Mt. 7:3.

3. CU, pp. 115-116.

4. DN, Book I, Chapter 3, Paragraph 1, p. 302.

5. CU, p. 107.

6. CU, p. 106.

7. DN, Book I, Chapter 4, Paragraph 5, p. 305.

8. DN, Book I, Chapter 4, Paragraph 7, p. 305.

9. WP, pp. 54-55.

10. DN, Book I, Chapter 6, Paragraph 1, p. 307.

11. CU, pp. 106-107.

12. DN, Book I, Chapter 6, Paragraph 7, p. 309.

13. DN, Book I, Chapter 6, Paragraph 8, p. 309.

14. Mt. 6:11-12.

15. Lk. 15:7.

16. Mt. 18:22.

17. See Mt. 20:23-35.

18. Mt. 20:35.

19. L, 19, p. 699. To Dona Juana de Pedraza, in Granada, Segovia, October 12, 1589.

20. Lk. 23:34.

CHAPTER FIVE

BLESSING OF AFFLICTION

1. See *Light Upon the Scaffold: The Prison Letters of Jacques Fesch,* ed. Augustin-Michel Lemonnier (St. Meinrad, Ind.: Abbey Press, 1975). Hereafter abbreviation LS.

2. See LS, p. 45.

3. See DN, Book II, Chapter 5, pp. 335-337.

4. LS, p. 80.

5. LS, p. 86.

6. DN, Book II, Chapter 5, Paragraph 5, p. 336.

7. LS, p. 70. In a letter from Jacques to his friend who has just been ordained a priest, he writes:

Where do you find such love and strength, dear brother? Right now, I'm like a rag, so low in my courage and fervor, "for my days have vanished like smoke, and my bones have dried up like wood in the fire." You are right, dear brother: this long period of dryness is certainly more profitable to me spiritually. But, Lord! It's hard! "I have no peace nor ease; I have no rest, for trouble comes!" (Jb. 3:26), and God's seeming desertion of me disconcerts me. I have the feeling of being abandoned and left to my own resources; I am horrified to see that everything I thought was far behind me and forever gone from me is at the door of my soul. The same evil thoughts as virulent as they were before my conversion, assail me as strongly as ever; they attract my mind and I need all my strength to overcome them.

Jacques realizes that temptations are necessary for our humility: "otherwise we would fall into a pleasant doze." See LS, p. 71.

8. LS, p. 132. Author's italics.

9. All my dearest friends recoil from me in horror:
      those I loved best have turned against me,
   Beneath my skin, my flesh begins to rot,
      and my bones stick out like teeth.
   Pity me, pity me, you, my friends,
      for the hand of God has struck me.
   Why do you hound me down like God,
      will you never have enough of my flesh?

                                           Jb. 19:19-22

10. DN, Book II, Chapter 6, Paragraph 1, p. 337.

11. LS, p. 63.

12. DN, Book II, Chapter 6, Paragraph 5, p. 339.

13. DN, Book II, Chapter 6, Paragraph 5, p. 339.

14. LS, p. 60. Jacques quotes Romans 7:22-24: " . . . What a wretched man I am! Who can free me from this body under the power of death?"

15. DN, Book II, Chapter 6, Paragraph 6, p. 339.

16. DN, Book II, Chapter 7, Paragraph 4, p. 342.

17. LS, p. 61.

18. LS, p. 54.

19. DN, Book II, Chapter 7, Paragraph 7, p. 343.

20. DN, Book II, Chapter 7, Paragraph 3, p. 341.

21. DN, Book II, Chapter 8, Paragraph 1, p. 343.

22. LS, p. 38.

23. DN, Stanza 3 and Stanza 5, pp. 295-296.

24. DN, Book II, Chapter 9, Paragraph 1, p. 346. In Book I, Chapters 12 and 13, pp. 320-327, St. John explains the benefits of the dark night of sense and in Book II, Chapters 11 to 13, pp. 352-361, he considers many delightful effects of the dark night of spirit.

25. LS, p. 121. Author's italics.

26. Lk. 1:46-47 as quoted in LS, p. 118.

27. See LS, Chapter 12, pp. 127-138.

28. LS, p. 132.

29. LS, p. 133. Author's italics.

30. Lk. 23:43 as quoted in LS, p. 145.

31. LS, p. 149.

32. LS, p. 149.

33. LS, p. 150.

34. ML, 8, p. 674; 13, p. 675; and 23, p. 675.

35. LFL, Stanza 2, p. 595.

CHAPTER SIX

TASTING ETERNAL HAPPINESS

1. See AMC, Book I, Chapter 4, pp. 77-81.

2. AMC, Book I, Chapter 13, Paragraph 11, p. 103.

3. See Lk. 2:25-35.

4. T.S. Eliot, "A Song for Simeon," in *The Complete Poems and Plays,* 1909-1950 (New York: Harcourt, Brace & World, 1934), pp. 69-70.

5. Lk. 2:29-32.

6. LS, p. 151.

7. See DN, Book II, Chapters 17 to 20, pp. 368-378.

8. DN, Book II, Chapter 20, Paragraph 2, p. 376.

9. DN, Book II, Chapter 20, Paragraph 2, p. 376.

10. DN, Book II, Chapter 20, Paragraph 4, p. 377.

11. LS, p. 145.

12. DN, Book II, Chapter 20, Paragraph 5, p. 377.

13. L, 14, p. 696. To Madre Leonor de San Gabriel, Discalced Carmelite in Cordoba, Segovia, July 8, 1589.

14. L, 16, p. 697. To Madre Maria de Jesus, Prioress of the Discalced Carmelites in Cordoba, Segovia, July 18, 1589.

15. See Corrie Ten Boom, *The Hiding Place.*

EPILOGUE

1. He conveys this important knowledge in LFL, Stanza 3, Paragraphs 27 to 67, pp. 620-637.

2. LFL, Stanza 3, Paragraph 30, p. 621.

3. LFL, Stanza 3, Paragraph 30, p. 621.

4. LFL, Stanza 3, Paragraph 38, pp. 624-625.

5. LFL, Stanza 3, Paragraph 43, p. 626.

6. LFL, Stanza 3, Paragraph 43, p. 626.

7. LFL, Stanza 3, Paragraph 45, p. 627.

8. LFL, Stanza 3, Paragraph 54, p. 621.

9. LFL, Stanza 3, Paragraph 57, p. 632.

10. LFL, Stanza 3, Paragraph 65, p. 636.

11. LFL, Stanza 3, Paragraph 66, p. 636.

12. LFL, Stanza 3, Paragraph 46, pp. 627-628.

13. LFL, Stanza 3, p. 610.

14. LFL, Stanza 3, Paragraph 12, p. 615.

SELECTED BIBLIOGRAPHY*

a Kempis, Thomas. *The Imitation of Christ*. Trans. Ronald Knox and Michael Oakley. New York: Sheed and Ward, 1960.

Anonymous. *The Cloud of Unknowing* and *The Book of Privy Counseling*. Ed. William Johnston. Garden City, N.Y.: Doubleday & Co., Image Books, 1973.

Bernard of Clairvaux, St. *Treatises II*. Trans. M. Ambrose Conway and Robert Walton. Washington, D.C.: Cistercian Publications Consortium Press, 1974.

Ciszek, Walter J. with Daniel L. Flaherty. *He Leadeth Me*. Garden City, N.Y.: Doubleday & Co., 1973.

Delp, Alfred. *The Prison Meditations of Father Alfred Delp*. New York: The Macmillan Co., 1963.

Egan, Keith J. "Giugo II: The Theology of the Contemplative Life." *The Spirituality of Western Christendom*. Ed. E. Rozanne Elder. Kalamazoo, Mich.: Cistercian Publications, 1976, pp. 106-115.

*For an extensive bibliography to the literature of spirituality, see *A Practical Guide to Spiritual Reading*, pp. 178-243.

Eliot, T.S. *The Complete Poems and Plays,* 1909-1950. New York: Harcourt, Brace & World, 1934.

Fedotov, G.P. *The Russian Religious Mind.* Two Volumes. Ed. John Meyendorff. Cambridge, Mass.: Harvard University Press, 1966.

Fesch, Jacques. *Light Upon the Scaffold: The Prison Letters of Jacques Fesch.* Ed. Augustin-Michel Lemonier. St. Meinrad, Ind.: Abbey Press, 1975.

Franck, Frederick. *The Zen of Seeing: Seeing/Drawing as Meditation.* New York: Vintage Books, 1973.

Frank, Anne, *The Diary of a Young Girl.* Trans. B.M. Mooyaart-Doubleday. New York: The Modern Library, 1952.

Hurnard, Hannah. *Hinds' Feet on High Places.* Old Tappan, N.J.: Fleming H. Revell Co., 1973.

——————. *Hearing Heart.* London: The Olive Press, 1952.

John of the Cross, St. *The Collected Works of St. John of the Cross.* Trans. Kieran Kavanaugh and Otilio Rodriguez. Washington, D.C.: Institute of Carmelite Studies, 1973.

Libermann, Francis. *Spiritual Letters to Clergy and Religious.* Volume Two. Pittsburgh, Pa.: Duquesne University Press, 1964.

Merton, Thomas. *The Ascent to Truth.* New York: The Viking Press, Compass Books, 1959.

_____. *Disputed Questions.* New York: The New American Library, A Mentor-Omega Book, 1965.

Muto, Susan Annette. *Approaching the Sacred: An Introduction to Spiritual Reading.* Denville, N.J.: Dimension Books, 1973.

_____. *Steps Along the Way: The Path of Spiritual Reading.* Denville, N.J.: Dimension Books, 1975.

_____. *A Practical Guide to Spiritual Reading.* Denville, N.J.: Dimension Books, 1976.

Rahner, Karl. "Reflections on the Problem of the Gradual Ascent to Christian Perfection." *Theological Investigations.* Volume III. "The Theology of the Spiritual Life." Trans. Karl H. and Boniface Kruger. New York: The Seabury Press, 1974, pp. 3-23.

Solzhenitsyn, Alexander. *One Day in the Life of Ivan Denisovich.* New York: Bantam Books, 1963.

_____. *The First Circle.* New York: Bantam Books, 1969.

ten Boom, Corrie. *The Hiding Place.* London: Hodder and Stoughton, 1971.

_____. *Tramp for the Lord.* New York: Pillar Books, 1976.

Teresa of Avila, St. *The Collected Works of St. Teresa of Avila.* Volume One. Trans. Kieran Kavanaugh and Otilio Rodriguez. Washington, D.C.: Institute of Carmelite Studies, ICS Publications, 1976.

_____. *The Way of Perfection.* Trans. E. Allison Peers. Garden City, N.Y.: Doubleday & Co., Image Books, 1964.

van Kaam, Adrian. *In Search of Spiritual Identity.* Denville, N.J.: Dimension Books, 1975.

_____. *The Dynamics of Spiritual Self Direction.* Denville, N.J.: Dimension Books, 1976.

von Dürckheim, Karlfried Graf. *Daily Life as Spiritual Exercise: The Way of Transformation.* Trans. Ruth Lewinneck and P.L. Travers. New York: Harper & Row, Publishers, Perennial Library, 1972.

_____. *Hara, The Vital Centre of Man.* Trans. Sylvia-Monica von Kospoth. New York: Fernhill House, 1962.

_____. *The Japanese Cult of Tranquility.* Trans. Eda O'Shiel, London: Rider & Company, 1960.

von Hügel, Baron Friedrich. *Letters from Baron Friedrich von Hügel to a Niece.* Ed. Gwendolen Greene. London: J.M. Dent & Sons, 1928.

Weil, Simone. *Waiting for God.* Trans. Emma Craufurd. New York: Harper & Row, Publishers, Harper Colophon Books, 1973.